Electronic
Eros

ELECTRONIC Eros

Bodies

and

Desire

in the

Postindustrial

Age

by Claudia
Springer

University of Texas Press
Austin

Grateful acknowledgment is made to the following for permission to reproduce material originally appearing in their publications:

"The Pleasure of the Interface" in Screen *32:3 (1991); "Muscular Circuitry: The Invincible Armored Cyborg in Cinema" in* Genders *#18 (Winter 1993); "Men and Machine-Women" in* Now Time *#3 (1993); "Sex, Memories, and Angry Women" in* South Atlantic Quarterly *92:4 (Fall 1993).*

∞ *The paper used in this publication meets the minimum requirements of American National Standard for Information Sciences — Permanence of Paper for Printed Library Materials,* ANSI Z39.48-1984.

Library of Congress Cataloging-in-Publication Data

Springer, Claudia, 1956–
   Electronic eros : bodies and desire in the postindustrial age / Claudia Springer. — 1st ed.
       p.   cm.
   Includes bibliographical references and index.
   ISBN 0-292-77696-9 (cloth : alk. paper)
   ISBN 0-292-77697-7 (pbk. : alk. paper)
   1. Mass media and technology.   2. Cyborgs in mass media.   3. Sex in mass media. 4. Erotica.   I. Title.
P96.T42S67   1996   95-36454
302.23 — dc20

For
Geoff
and
Jack

CONTENTS

ix Acknowledgments

3 Introduction
Techno-Eroticism

16 Chapter One
Deleting the Body

50 Chapter Two
The Pleasure of the Interface

80 Chapter Three
Virtual Sex

95 Chapter Four
Muscular Circuitry

125 Chapter Five
Digital Rage

146 Chapter Six
Men and Machine-Women

162 Notes

174 Index

ACKNOWLEDGMENTS

I EXTEND MY GRATITUDE to the comic book aficionados who originally inspired me to begin this project. The book has benefited enormously from the contributions and support of many people over the course of several years. Some wrote careful critiques of the manuscript, others helped to shape the material I published as articles, and still others brought to my attention relevant texts that I had overlooked. I am grateful also to friends, colleagues, and students who have given me their enthusiastic support: Thanks to Annette Kuhn, Claudia Gorbman, Sarelle Reid, Miyoshi Barosh, Rick Berg, Chuck Kleinhans, Thomas Foster, Scott Bukatman,

James D. Hudnall, Spencer Hall, Justin Hall, David Ripley, Gary Whitehead, George Adams, Barbara Schapiro, Lynne Layton, Joan Dagle, Kathryn Kalinak, Virginia Keller, Richard Weiner, Harriet Brisson, Cathy Calbert, Barbara Mortimer, and Chris Straayer.

With special thanks I acknowledge the invaluable assistance of Vivian Sobchack and Mark Dery, both of whom went above and beyond the call of duty to provide me with detailed suggestions for revision.

I wish to thank Joanna Hitchcock, Tayron Tolley Cutter, Leslie Tingle, and Bruce Bethell at the University of Texas Press for their integrity and efficiency.

My parents and brothers—George, Annemarie, Lenny, and Joel Springer—have provided me not only with familial support but also with information about pertinent texts and perceptive responses to my published articles.

Above all, I thank Geoff Adams for his kindness, patience, intelligence, and sense of humor, which made the discouraging moments bearable and the writing process infinitely more enjoyable.

Electronic
Eros

INTRODUCTION

Techno-Eroticism

AT THE INTERSECTION of technology and eroticism lies techno-eroticism, the passionate celebration of technological objects of desire. Artistic renderings of technology since the early twentieth century have often expressed techno-erotic impulses. Italian futurism, for example, fetishized the speed and powerful force of industrial machines from about 1909 until 1914, when World War I revealed the monstrously destructive aspect of technology and ended the lives of several futurist artists. Social commentators have detected a heavy dose of techno-eroticism running throughout twentieth-century Western culture. As film scholar K. C. D'Alessandro writes:

*Sexual metaphor in the description of
locomotives, automobiles, pistons, and turbines;
machine cults and the Futurist movement,* Man
with a Movie Camera, *and* Scorpio Rising—
*these are some of the ways technophiliacs have
expressed their passion for technology. For
technophiliacs, technology provides an erotic
thrill—control over massive power, which can
itself be used to control others. . . . The physical
manifestations of these machines—size, heft,
shape, motions that thrust, pause and press
again—represent human sexual responses on a
grand scale. There is much to venerate in the
technology of the Industrial age.*[1]

Industrial-age techno-eroticism focused in particular on the automobile, an object of fascination for generations. Cars represent the culmination of industrial technology, combining engines, gears, wheels, and chrome into a beautifully streamlined device, extending and transforming the human body so that it can experience exhilarating blasts of speed and power. Industrial technology still surrounds us, but it has been superseded in the late twentieth century by the miniaturized intricacy of electronic circuitry. Gasoline-powered cars now have the aura of outdated relics from another age; computers are the current pinnacle of industrial achievement. As an object of erotic attraction, electronic technology is of a different order from the industrial technology exemplified by the car. Whereas industrial technology has robust physical presence and moves visibly through space, the workings of computers and other electronic equipment are encased within plastic boxes and hidden behind opaque screens. Additionally, the glory of industrial technology was its enormousness combined with power; enthusiasts were transfixed by big, bold, and fast machines. Electronic technology, in contrast, is dwindling in size; personal computers, for example, are becoming increasingly portable and inconspicuous. These postindustrial "machines of reproduction rather than of production," in the words of Fredric Jameson, do not have the same forceful presence as their industrial forebears. Jameson observes:

What must then immediately be observed is that the technology of our own moment no longer possesses this same capacity for representation: not the turbine, nor even Sheeler's grain elevators or smokestacks, not the baroque elaboration of pipes and conveyor belts nor even the stream-lined profile of the railroad train—all vehicles of speed still concentrated at rest—but rather the computer, whose outer shell has no emblematic or visual power, or even the casings of the various media themselves, as with that home appliance called television which articulates nothing but rather implodes, carrying its flattened image surface within itself.[2]

In many ways industrial technology and postindustrial electronic technology are complete opposites.

Perhaps the apotheosis of techno-erotic fascination with the car, that icon of industrial achievement, is the science-fiction novel *Crash* by J. G. Ballard.[3] Ballard's ironic commentary on the sterile industrial landscape's effects on human fantasies and desires takes the cult of the automobile to its extreme. The novel's narrator, "Ballard," is injured in a car accident that kills one of the occupants of the other vehicle. After his release from the hospital, he falls under the influence of Vaughan, also a scarred survivor of a car wreck, who has developed a sexual obsession with car accidents and the erotic possibilities of twisted metal and injured bodies. Together, Vaughan and "Ballard" cruise the highways and roads neighboring an airport. Surrounded by concrete and steel, they seek out car crashes in order to watch the grisly aftermath. They engage in backseat sex with prostitutes, crash survivors, and eventually each other, but their sexual acts are described in the dry and precise prose of a technical manual, inspired by the technological sterility surrounding them. Although the narrator is transformed by his accident, developing a fascination with chrome and wounds, his attraction to mechanical forms already existed; he describes his wife as if she were made of plastic or chrome rather than flesh and explains that her inhumanly smooth perfection has always been the source of his attraction.[4]

The inevitable climax of the novel's fusion of sexuality and technology is death. Vaughan meticulously rehearses his own death in a car accident, planning also to take the life of actress Elizabeth Taylor by crashing into her limousine, joining their bodies in a mangled embrace. He fails to kill Taylor but in the attempt crashes into a bus, killing himself and a number of the bus's passengers. The novel's narrator indicates that Vaughan viewed his death as part of Western society's collective collision course: "In his mind Vaughan saw the whole world dying in a simultaneous automobile disaster, millions of vehicles hurled together in a terminal congress of spurting loins and engine coolant."[5]

J. G. Ballard recounts in an interview that a psychiatrist responding to *Crash* pronounced the author seriously disturbed "beyond psychiatric help."[6] The psychiatrist failed to detect the novel's ironic and moralistic tone. Ballard explored the depths of techno-eroticism in *Crash* not because he recommended it to his readers but because he was concerned about transformations to the human psyche brought about by an increasingly sterile and meaningless world. As he writes in his introduction to the French edition, "Throughout *Crash* I have used the car not only as a sexual image, but as a total metaphor for man's life in today's society. . . . Needless to say, the ultimate role of *Crash* is cautionary, a warning against that brutal, erotic and overlit realm that beckons more and more persuasively to us from the margins of the technological landscape."[7]

In an essay on *Crash* Jean Baudrillard dismisses Ballard's claim that the book was written as a warning. In Baudrillard's reading the novel is unique because it avoids all morality, psychology, and conventional ideas about sexuality and achieves a hyperreality that surpasses all distinctions between reality and simulation.[8] Baudrillard's position on *Crash*, however, has been criticized by some of the leading figures in science-fiction scholarship. According to N. Katherine Hayles, Baudrillard misperceives and misreads the novel, failing to observe obvious borders between reality and simulation and therefore enacting, rather than simply describing, the implosion into simulation. In addition, writes Hayles, Baudrillard ignores the novel's motif of flight, which evokes the desire for transcendence through death; Vaughan achieves this when his car lifts off the ground for a moment before crashing into a bus and killing him.[9]

Film theorist Vivian Sobchack joins Hayles in insisting on Ballard's moralistic stance in *Crash*. She writes that "Ballard's vision sees this techno-body as driving us, quite literally, to a dead end." She sums up the difference between Ballard's and Baudrillard's tones: "Thus where Ballard is ironic and chillingly reductive in limning the postmodern desire to 'come' into the machine, to convert the male body's 'software' into 'hardware,' Baudrillard is celebratory and chillingly expansive." Sobchack writes that her own experience with severe physical pain (a series of leg operations) has reinforced for her the importance of writing with the awareness of one's own body and subjectivity: "If we don't keep this subjective kind of bodily sense in mind as we negotiate our technoculture, then we, like Vaughan, like Baudrillard, will objectify ourselves to death."[10] Sobchack's warning can apply to a range of recent writings on technology, particularly the effusive visions of liberation through human metamorphosis into machinery. In fact, in another essay Sobchack targets one magazine, *Mondo 2000*, for what she identifies as its clever but irresponsible technophilia.[11] From Baudrillard to *Mondo 2000*, those who adulate technology's penetration of the human body and mind can lose sight of how the attempt to become a technological object leads inevitably to extinction.

If anything, the marriage of technology and sexuality has become even more pervasive in popular imagery in the years since 1973, when Ballard wrote *Crash*. Ballard in fact anticipated the flourishing of techno-eroticism associated with new technologies when he wrote in *Crash*, "What wounds would create the sexual possibilities of the invisible technologies of thermonuclear reaction chambers, white-tiled control rooms, the mysterious scenarios of computer circuitry?"[12]

In this book I argue that the newer electronic technologies have inspired changes in techno-erotic imagery in some popular-culture texts but that other texts recycle techno-erotic conventions derived from Western society's industrial past, refusing to come to terms with the new postmodern social order and all the transformations it has brought. This book, informed by studies in the history of technology, analyzes techno-erotic imagery in recent films, fiction, comic books, television programs, and computer software, as well as scientific writing on artificial intelligence and other simulated life forms. It analyzes the tendency in popular culture to associate computer technology with sexuality, creating a contradictory discourse that simultaneously predicts the obsolescence of human beings and a future of heightened erotic fulfillment.

Technology has no sex, but representations of technology often do. Historians of technology have pointed out that new inventions have been accompanied by sexual impulses throughout history. John Tierney writes, "Sometimes the erotic has been a force driving technological innovation; virtually always, from Stone Age sculpture to computer bulletin boards, it has been one of the first uses for a new medium."[13] He traces the erotic technological drive back to its earliest incarnations:

The erotic technological impulse dates back at least to some of the earliest works of art, the so-called Venus figurines of women with exaggerated breasts and buttocks, which were made by firing clay 27,000 years ago—15 millenniums before ceramics technology was used for anything utilitarian like pots. When subsequent artists discovered the medium of cave walls, they produced work like the rock

carving that archeologists have titled "Nude
Woman," etched more than 12,000 years ago
at La Magdelaine Cave in France.

Tierney goes on to state that "the oldest known literature, recorded by the Sumerians in cuneiform on clay tablets, includes poetry celebrating the sweetness of a woman's lips and vulva." He documents the use of communications media for sexual expression from the invention of the printing press to the introduction of the novel, photography, films, videocassette recorders, computers, and pay-per-call telephone services. Tierney's analysis illustrates that the histories of technology and the erotic are closely linked.

Mechanical objects have been imbued with male or female sexual characteristics for centuries; consequently, representations of machines long have been used to express ideas about sexual identity and gender roles. Machines from the industrial age were often described in gendered terms, frequently associating their forceful energy with virile masculinity. Not all powerful mechanical objects were perceived as masculine, however. Ships and boats, for example, were and still are often engendered as female, implying a sexual tension with their crews and evoking notions of physical beauty as well as maternal safety and comfort.

The industrial-age tendency to apply gendered metaphors to machines continues in the electronic age but is complicated by the computer's ambiguous relationship to gender. The design of a computer does not immediately evoke either male or female attributes; if anything, it presents a bland and asexual surface. But the urge to assign a gender to machines persists. Consequently, in an attempt to masculinize their products, manufacturers refer to their computers' power and strength, and magazine advertisements compare computers to rugged motorcycles. At the same time, however, other computer enthusiasts invest computers with attributes they consider feminine: small size, fluid and quiet functioning, and the ability to absorb the user's ego in an empathic bond. Still others celebrate the computer's supposed gender-bending capabilities that allow users to create their on-line personae: men can become women and vice versa.

There is no consensus, then, on the computer's metaphoric gender, but there is cultural acceptance of the idea that computers can be gendered. What the various contradictory gendered metaphors make apparent is that computer discourses incorporate current cultural debates over men's and women's roles. Conflicting viewpoints about gender roles that are dividing Western society into polarized camps surface in unexpected contexts, infiltrating even the language people use to discuss their machines.

In this book I look at fictional representations of cyborgs—cybernetic organisms—which are part human and part machine, representing the increasing integration of human beings with their technology. I argue that popular culture plays out contemporary cultural conflicts over sexuality and gender roles in its representation of cyborgs. Although technology has been radically transformed over the course of the twentieth century, from massive industrial machines to tiny microelectronic circuitry, representations of cyborgs often cling to an anachronistic concept of the invincible armored man of steel. This figure functions metaphorically to ward off the "feminization" of technology and culture. Phallic industrial imagery circulates alongside other imagery that celebrates the miniaturization and internalization of electronic technology. What results is a popular culture arena where cultural debates over sexuality and gender are played out in both literal and metaphoric guise. Debates about what it means to be male or female and how sexuality should be expressed often find their way into popular culture's techno-erotic imagery. The imagery sometimes explores alternative types of sexuality and gender roles and at other times retreats to conventional stereotypes from the past. Moreover, with the specter of AIDS surrounding us, there is the constant presence of death, as science and science fiction alike contemplate the extinction of human beings and the dispersion of human desires into a computerized electronic realm.

In chapter 1, "Deleting the Body," I discuss science and science fiction that envision a future devoid of human beings. The posthuman future imagined in these texts would be populated instead by computerized artificial intelligences or other simulated life forms. Scientists pursuing the creation of artificial life describe their work as an attempt to preserve human intelligence, but skeptics argue that abandoning the human body is synonymous with destroying human beings. People have attempted to create synthetic humans for centuries, and myths, legends, and literature have imagined what it would be like for humans to interact with their artificial creations. Science-fiction literature, most recently in the subgenre of cyberpunk, has explored the ramifications of technological transformation on the human mind and body. What emerges from both science and recent science fiction concerned with a posthuman future is ambivalence about the possibility of human survival given the threats of extinction facing humans today. Cyberpunk paints a bleak picture of an inhospitably technological world governed by ruthless, profit-driven corporations. Nonetheless, despite the dystopian visions, there is also a sense of excitement associated with technology in both science and cyberpunk. Giving human beings the ability to alter themselves technologically in any conceivable way creates an unstable, unpredictable world where people experience their most pleasurable fantasies and, in the next moment, their worst nightmares. Postmodern instability is taken to its extreme; nothing is necessarily what it seems, and illusion is the new reality.

In chapter 2, "The Pleasure of the Interface," I examine the tendency to associate computer technology with sexuality and the consequent contradictory discourses that predict both the obsolescence of human beings and heightened sexual satisfaction. Abandoning the body to exist within the computer matrix—in cyberspace—often holds out the promise of enhanced sexuality in popular culture. Even though cerebral sex replaces bodily contact in cyberspace, gender roles tend for the most part to remain stereotypical. Sexual identity can be altered, but the roles assigned to men and women, whether they are biologically or technologically created, are usually conventional in most cyberpunk texts. This has led some critics to accuse cyberpunk of rejecting the more provocative and experimental feminist science fiction from the 1960s and 1970s, when authors Joanna Russ and Ursula LeGuin, among others, challenged conventional gender categories. In cyberpunk and other techno-erotic texts from the 1980s and 1990s, conventions are both overturned and reestablished. Sexuality and gender are freed from biological constraints when they enter the domain of technology, but cultural conventions continue to exert an influence on how scientists and cyberpunk authors imagine their future worlds. As it was in Ballard's *Crash*, death is always in close proximity when the topic is human fusion with electronic technology. Creation versus destruction of life is a central theme in these works, which express fascination with the idea of oblivion while also fearing its irrevocability.

In chapter 3, "Virtual Sex," I analyze how erotic fantasies are a prominent feature of plans for the new illusionistic medium of virtual reality (VR). VR is not the first technological medium to come into existence amid speculation about its potential for providing sexual gratification, but debates over how it should be designed reveal diametrically opposed ways of thinking about the future of gender roles and sexual expression. One commentator expresses the desire to maintain conventional patriarchal regulations in the new virtual frontier, while another hopes that virtual reality will release men and women from the rigid roles that have stifled them. Popular culture, particularly in films, participates in linking virtual reality with prescriptions for gender roles and sexual expression.

In chapter 4, "Muscular Circuitry," I analyze the figure of the invincible armored cyborg in cinema, in particular the characters RoboCop and the Terminator. Although cyberpunk fiction and comic books have expressed some playful and imaginative ways to conceptualize cyborgs, mainstream Hollywood films privilege the figure of the aggressive killer. This fortified figure represents an anachronistic tendency to use masculine metaphors for technology. Although the man of steel was an understandable metaphor for forceful and aggressive industrial machinery, it is no longer appropriate for today's smaller, internalized electronic technology. The masculinist cybernetic figure in Hollywood films represents an attempt to ward off the mystery and miniaturization of technology and feminist changes in society. The films in which the figure of the invincible armored cyborg appears are not entirely consistent, however, for narrative contradictions and tensions undermine his supremacy. A film that presents an armored female cyborg, *Eve of Destruction* (Gibbins 1991), highlights the contradictions underlying Hollywood's depiction of mechanical humans; its feminist theme of a woman's rage against abusive men is clearly counteracted by a recuperative closure. The imagery and themes associated with invincible armored cyborgs in films have grown so familiar that they have become the object of parody.

In chapter 5, "Digital Rage," I discuss the ways in which humans and computers are discursively linked by theories positing that they function similarly. It is common for both computer scientists and cognitive psychologists to describe the human brain as if it were a computer and vice versa, thereby reducing the complexities of the human mind. Furthermore, there is a widespread cultural tendency to anthropomorphize computers. Cyberpunk fiction explores what might result from a truly digital existence, when the human mind could be copied and manipulated as if it were computer software. Despite its analogies between computers and the human brain, however, cyberpunk continues to depend on a Freudian model of complex human consciousness for its characterizations. Repressed memories and rage against sexual abuse figure prominently in cyborg films and cyberpunk fiction, in particular in the cyborg RoboCop and in the figure of the angry cybernetically enhanced woman warrior. The female techno-assassin has become a cyberpunk icon. Her appeal exists on at least two levels: on the one hand she is a fetishized male fantasy with a steely hard body, and on the other hand she is a feminist fighter who exhibits complete independence from patriarchal constraints. It is in her characterization, too, that cyberpunk reveals the ineffectiveness of the analogy between computers and human minds. As one novel, *Lady El*, makes clear, complex and contradictory human concerns inevitably continue to haunt cyborgs even after they have embraced a computerized existence.[14]

In chapter 6, "Men and Machine-Women," I compare two representations of machine-women, one from the early part of the twentieth century and one from the late part. The robot Maria in Fritz Lang's film *Metropolis* (1926) represents patriarchal fear of female sexuality and technology running out of control. Order can be restored to the futuristic city of Metropolis only when the lascivious robot is burned at the stake. A recent fictional machine-woman, Eve, in the NBC television series *Mann and Machine*, which aired in the spring of 1992, is depicted as the product of a society in which, unlike in that of *Metropolis*, women are in positions of power. Moreover Eve, unlike Maria, is naïve and innocent, requiring guidance from her male partner on the futuristic Los Angeles police force. Their interactions and the postmodern milieu around them illustrate how Western industrialized society has changed over the course of the century. Despite the feminist strides acknowledged by the series, however, there is still an attempt to impose conventional and inappropriate ideas about masculinity and femininity. The contradictory messages about gender roles that emerge from the series are signs that patriarchal ideology in the late twentieth century is no longer coherent or consistent and cannot hide the cracks in its reasoning.

Comic books, fiction, magazines, films, television programs, and computer software are analyzed here, but the selection is by no means exhaustive. There are countless examples of the phenomena under discussion circulating throughout contemporary culture. I have chosen to concentrate on those that are exemplary rather than try to include every example. A completely exhaustive summary, in any event, would be doomed to fail.

My analysis of popular culture in this book is informed by theories of postmodernism, feminist theory, psychoanalytic theory, and film theory. I have tried to be precise with terms derived from these theories, but some of them warrant a more complete explanation. I use the term *patriarchal* to refer to what Chris Weedon calls "power relations in which women's interests are subordinated to the interests of men."[15] She continues, "These power relations take many forms, from the sexual division of labour and the social organization of procreation to the internalized norms of femininity by which we live. Patriarchal power rests on the social meanings given to biological sexual difference. In patriarchal discourse the nature and social role of women are defined in relation to a norm which is male."[16]

Late-twentieth-century Western culture is no longer as rigidly patriarchal as it was during the Victorian era, but patriarchal traditions die hard and still dominate social and institutional practices, as well as ways of thinking about what it means to be male or female. I use the term *gender* to refer to the categories of "man" and "woman," which carry cultural connotations not inherent in a person's sex. Not all children born female grow up to fit comfortably within the parameters of what is commonly thought to be appropriate for women, but there are social pressures to conform to those parameters. The same is true for males, who are equally pressured to adopt cultural norms for manhood. Feminism, as it is used in this book, is a philosophy that seeks to end patriarchy and institute in its place an egalitarian system. Feminism seeks to release all people, men and women, from narrowly defined ideas about gender roles.

I use the word *technology* to refer to nonorganic crafts, tools, and machines created by humans. My use of the word encompasses mechanical, industrial, and electronic technology, but not biotechnology. I try in this book to make connections between ways of thinking in different disciplines in order to get a grasp on how people in the late twentieth century contemplate the future of humanity. Both the enthusiastic celebrations and the passionate denunciations of the technologically enhanced human are attempts to envision existence in the rapidly approaching twenty-first century. Change is imminent, and its unknown nature has produced utopian as well as colossally destructive fantasies. Although it is easy to be horrified by scientific texts that coolly and dispassionately discuss replacing human beings with technology, the prospect might not seem as repugnant to someone suffering from a debilitating illness that destroys bodies but leaves minds untouched. Above all, by examining people's ideas about the future, we can learn about their responses to present-day issues, for contemporary cultural battles find expression in even the most shocking and improbable speculations about the future.

CHAPTER 1

Deleting the Body

Can
thought
go on
without
a body?

Jean-François Lyotard[1]

W HEN RENÉ DESCARTES compared human beings to machines in the year 1637, he maintained that humans would always be superior to machines because humans possess the unique ability to reason. He wrote that although "machines could do many things as well as, or perhaps even better than, men, they would infallibly fail in certain others, by which we would discover that they did not act by understanding or reason, but only by the disposition of their organs."[2] In 1992 Steven Levy, writing about research into computerized "artificial life," identified the quality that he perceived as uniquely human: "Our uniqueness will lie in the ability to create our successors."[3] In the years between 1637 and 1992 human reason undertook the pursuit of making itself obsolete.

The seventeenth and eighteenth centuries bequeathed to subsequent generations a belief in the uniqueness of human beings. Humans, according to Enlightenment philosophy, are blessed with reason and thus enjoy superiority over animals and human-made artifacts. Enlightenment thinkers believed that reason gives humans the ability to create a better world rather than submit to a fixed social order and a preordained destiny. This belief in the power of human reason to control the environment culminated in the nineteenth-century Industrial Revolution. By harnessing machine force industrialists displayed the power of human intelligence over the brute strength of machines.

During the height of industrialization, however, in the late nineteenth century, perceptions of the relationship between humans and machines changed. Machines were increasingly described as superior to the human body.

With the coming of the industrial revolution and our entry into the machine age, the Victorians were forced to address the interface between the human and the machine in terms very different from those employed by Descartes. Political economists of the era extolled the virtues of the machine which seemed to offer a corrective to the inefficiency and indiscipline of human labor, endowing machines with the agency and productive powers previously assigned only to human life.[4]

A shift had occurred in how humans were differentiated from machines. For the Victorian proponents of industrialization, for whom human bodies constituted first and foremost an exploitable labor force, machines improved on what they saw as the deficiencies of human workers. Work-

FIG. 1. The cyborg Terminator in the film
The Terminator.

ers and machines were often discursively interchangeable: machines were
described as if they were human, and humans were characterized as fundamentally mechanical.

In the late twentieth century the distinction between human beings
and machines has become even more blurred. Human dependence on
technology has started to efface the line between the two. It has become
common for people to identify with machines and describe themselves as
machinelike, a phenomenon analyzed by both psychologist Sherry Turkle[5]
and historian of science J. David Bolter, who refers to the late-twentieth-
century human as "Turing's Man."[6] The idea of human interchangeabil-
ity with machines has been pushed even further by those who imagine
that humans and machines are merging to form a new hybrid entity: a
cybernetic organism, or cyborg. The figure of the cyborg—part human
and part machine—is now common in fiction, films, television, comic
books, magazines, computer games, and video games and can also be
found in the works of scientists and contemporary cultural theorists.

FIG. 2. The cyborg RoboCop in the film *RoboCop*.

The idea of the cyborg is simultaneously a culmination of Descartes's separation of reason from emotion and a supersession of that opposition. At the same time that the cyborg represents the triumph of the intellect, it also signifies obsolescence for human beings and the dawn of a posthuman, post-Enlightenment age. In other words, the cyborg appears to rest on a dichotomy between mind and body, but it actually supersedes the dichotomy and makes it anachronistic in a new vision of fusion and symbiosis with electronic technology.

There are several types of cyborgs represented in popular culture. Two of the most common types are defined by David Tomas, an artist and anthropologist at the University of Ottawa: "the post-organic . . . classical (hardware-interfaced) cyborg and the postclassical (software-interfaced) transorganic data-based cyborg or personality construct."[7] The first type combines the organic human body, which either preexisted as a person or was genetically engineered, with nonorganic mechanical or electronic implants or prostheses. The second type has no organic form but consists of the human mind preserved on computer software. When fictional characters load software directly into their electronically wired brains, they also qualify as cyborgs. Cyborgs differ from robots, which are completely mechanical figures of any shape or size. Cyborgs also differ from androids, which look like humans and sometimes are indistinguishable from them. Androids can be human-shaped robots or genetically engineered humanoid organisms, but they do not combine organic with nonorganic parts. The replicants in the film *Blade Runner* (Scott 1982) are therefore androids, not cyborgs, because they are genetically engineered organic entities and contain no nonbiological components. The terms *robot, android*, and *cyborg* generate a great deal of confusion and are sometimes mistakenly interchanged. It is only the cyborg, however, that represents the fusion of particular human beings with technology, an idea that resonates throughout contemporary culture.

Cyborgs have become a familiar part of the fictional landscape surrounding us. The Terminator and RoboCop, two cyborgs from popular films, have achieved the status of cultural icons; nearly everyone has heard of them, even people who have not seen the films that introduced them. The presence of cyborgs in our popular fiction and films is one aspect of a much larger field of discourses concerned with the nature of life in the future and with the possibility of human obsolescence.

Debates surrounding the future of human existence have become widespread in the last decades of the twentieth century. On one side, there are researchers and theorists who envision a future time when artificial beings with intelligence equal to or surpassing human intelligence will inhabit the Earth. The advent of simulated life, they explain, could put humans in a subordinate role or perhaps even establish a future devoid of human beings. They contend that the world will be populated by artificial intelligences, artificial electronic life, genetically engineered organisms, cybernetic organisms, or human consciousness preserved on computer software and stored in mobile robots. Working on widely disparate projects, researchers disagree about which procedures hold the most promise, and there are conflicting points of view even within particular fields, such as artificial intelligence (AI). There is also a widespread perception that the development of AI has failed to measure up to its proponents' early optimistic predictions and that other avenues of research into simulated life might produce more impressive results. There are computer scientists, for example, who are developing self-reproducing computer programs they call "artificial life." In his book *Artificial Life*, which documents the ideas and work of researchers who are pursuing the creation of such programs, Steven Levy explains that "artificial life, or a-life, is devoted to the creation and study of lifelike organisms and systems built by humans. The stuff of this life is nonorganic matter, and its essence is information: computers are the kilns from which these new organisms emerge. Just as medical scientists have managed to tinker with life's mechanisms in vitro, the biologists and computer scientists of a-life hope to create life in silico."[8]

One type of a-life that proponents perceive as a corrective to the limitations of traditional AI research is the neural network, which, as Maureen Caudill explains in *In Our Own Image*, "is quite different from the neatly compartmentalized design of a digital computer."[9] Neural network–style computers are designed to imitate the functions of the neurons in the human brain. Taking the idea even further, a scientist in Japan, Masuo Aizawa, is growing artificial nerve cells that he predicts will work better than the electronic devices used by computer scientists to mimic neural activity. Aizawa hopes that his experiments might eventually lead to the development of sophisticated biocomputers that marry biological to electronic components.[10]

Research into the different forms of simulated life has generated a great deal of enthusiasm. A proponent of AI, Pamela McCorduck, ends her book about its history, *Machines Who Think*, with the reverential lines, "The accomplishments have been significant, and the promises are nearly beyond comprehension. I pause just now, before I have to call forth fortitude and exhibit courage. I pause to savor the thrill of sharing in something awesome."[11] McCorduck shares with other enthusiasts the sense that human beings are at the dawn of a revolutionary new age. Hans

Moravec, director of the Mobile Robot Laboratory at Carnegie Mellon University, writes, "We are on a threshold of a change in the universe comparable to the transition from non-life to life."[12] He refers to the future he envisions as "postbiological" and explains:

Unleashed from the plodding pace of biological evolution, the children of our minds will be free to grow to confront immense and fundamental challenges in the larger universe. We humans will benefit for a time from their labors, but sooner or later, like natural children, they will seek their own fortunes while we, their aged parents, silently fade away. Very little need be lost in this passing of the torch—it will be in our artificial offspring's power, and to their benefit, to remember almost everything about us, even, perhaps, the detailed workings of individual human minds.[13]

Some observers are caught up in the enthusiasm generated by Moravec and other researchers into simulated life but are nevertheless uncomfortable with the implications of their research. In his book *The Tomorrow Makers: A Brave New World of Living-Brain Machines*, Grant Fjermedal describes his lengthy conversations with many of the foremost scientists involved in AI and robotics research, including Moravec. Fjermedal's fascination with their projects and ideas is tempered by concern about potentially disastrous results. He writes that "whenever science discovers a new tool, there seem to be ways to twist it away from goodness and employ it for evil." Possible scenarios he cites involve computer-controlled robots becoming totalitarian dictators over humans, forming a ruthless police force, unleashing a nuclear holocaust, or in the case of "bacteria-size robots," systematically destroying all life on Earth. "That," Fjermedal writes, "is the bad news."[14]

There are others who not only express discomfort with cataclysmic visions of the future but also voice grave misgivings about the claims made by proponents of simulated life. In his books *The Emperor's New Mind* and *Shadows of the Mind* Roger Penrose, professor of mathematics at the University of Oxford, launches a carefully detailed critique of the underlying precepts of AI research, addressing in particular the strong AI view that artificial intelligence can simulate perfectly the workings of the human mind. Penrose cites "the untenability of the viewpoint—apparently rather prevalent in current philosophizing—that our thinking is basically the same as the action of some very complicated computer."[15] He makes a case for his view that "true intelligence requires consciousness" and therefore cannot be simulated by a computer using purely algorithmic means.[16] What Penrose defends is an "essentially non-algorithmic ingredient in the action of consciousness" that cannot be imitated by any system that operates merely by computation.

Other critics of the pursuit of simulated life condemn the Cartesian mind/body duality that characterizes the scientific tradition, perceiving a direct link between the elevation of reason and an "antihuman" stance. Michael Blumlein, a physician and novelist, writes that "there are no road signs saying 'Brain' and 'Body,'" and he describes those who maintain the distinction as "victims of the fractured world view, the spurious duality of mind/body." As a practitioner of a holistic approach to health care, he writes, "I wage my battles against this way of thinking."[17] More bluntly, a peace activist named Starhawk wonders whether "the ability to turn cartwheels or have orgasms seems irrelevant to a roboticist."[18]

These debates have not taken place exclusively in a scientific ivory tower far removed from public notice. In their more esoteric forms ideas about posthuman life exist in specialized scientific works, but in a more accessible guise they circulate widely throughout contemporary popular culture, familiarizing the public with posthuman imagery. Science fiction has treated the concept of simulated life for decades, and the scientific creation of human life was a literary topic during the nineteenth century, when Mary Shelley wrote the best-known and most influential example,

Frankenstein (1818). The last ten or so years, however, have seen an explosion of interest.

In 1989, for example, the *Whole Earth Review* invited a selection of authors, scientists, artists, and scholars to respond to the question, "Is the body obsolete?" Their responses, published as a forum, reveal a wide range of opinions, including Blumlein's and Starhawk's previously quoted critiques of the idea of bodily obsolescence. The wide spectrum of responses in the forum reveals a cultural conflict over the value of human existence and the ethics of research into simulated life-forms. Enormous discrepancies emerge in what the respondents say they experience as the nature of human life; their responses are influenced by their individual interests and desires, and their opinions about artificial life are equally subjective.[19]

Author Kathy Acker rejects the notion of bodily obsolescence by likening it to suicide: "There's not much in this world I love, and among what I do and can love are my body and other people's bodies. I don't think I can even conceive of the body being obsolete unless I start thinking about suicide" (51). Acker's celebration of physical passion is echoed by feminist porn star Nina Hartley: "Anyone who has regular orgasms can tell you the absurdity of saying the body is obsolete" (41). Stephanie Mills, who has written on ecological issues, believes in the sanctity of the body, writing, "bodies are holy, right down to the asshole." She goes on to forge a link between patriarchal exploiters of women and workers throughout history and contemporary robotics researchers, whom she describes as "tall white guys with good teeth, the same crowd that for centuries has been dependent on the physical labor of wives, slaves, children, or laborers, proxy bodies regarded as being more dispensable than those of the father classes. An awful lot of overreaching was accomplished by these suffering proxies—cannon-fodder borne, looms tended, coal mined, rails laid, and towers flung up" (45). Mills's cultural critique is extended by Yaakov Garb, who at the time was a Ph.D. candidate studying the role emotions play in the development of scientific knowledge. He asks "why this kind of illusion emerges with such urgency in these times: who holds these fantasies, and what is it about our political, social, cultural and environmental condition that allows (and funds) them to entertain these latest incarnations of the longing for individual and global disembodiment?" He continues:

Why, for instance, are we so eager to disown the material substrates of our lives in a time when the fabric of our world—from soil to ozone layer—does actually feel like it is disintegrating? Why, as toxins and radiation trickle into the most fundamental recesses of our cells and ecosystems, is there such enthusiasm for self-sufficient space colonies, disembodied intellects, and cyborg futures? Why is etherealism so popular in a world where matter isn't? More eerily, how do the fantasies of disengagement from body and nature emerge from the same military/industrial complex which manufactures the technologies for the actual destruction of both? (53)

Author Susan Griffin provides a historical context for the question of bodily obsolescence by tracing a tradition of Western belief in the body's insignificance: "For centuries in this particular civilization, we have been behaving as if the body were obsolete. The Judeo-Christian ethic, especially after the Roman Empire became the Holy Roman Empire, categorizes bodily knowledge as evil. For over two millennia we have skated on the thin ice of a dangerous illusion: that spirit is excluded from matter" (52). The tradition of ignoring the body's profound presence, writes Griffin, has allowed world leaders to treat human bodies as expendable during wartime. She concludes that we have hardly begun to discover our bodies, since we have long been stifled and constrained by authoritarian strictures.

A personal response comes from Mark O'Brien, a writer whose bout with polio at age six left his body disabled and his lungs unable to breathe on their own for more than an hour. He spends most of his life inside a

900-pound iron lung. Unlike the respondents who reject obsolescence by extolling bodily pleasures, O'Brien identifies consciousness as the principal human characteristic worth preserving. He writes that he would welcome the greater mobility he could achieve with a smaller, lighter iron lung, but he would be interested in such a device only if it were controlled by his consciousness. He writes, "our impulse to invent has come from a desire to supplement our strength or our senses. Even now that we have computers to handle information faster than human consciousness could, we don't relinquish the overall direction of these computers" (36). O'Brien has no interest in a machine that would rob him of the ability to make his own decisions: "I'm not a powerful person, but I am not about to surrender the power of conscious direction, the one power left to me. If I get a dream-machine iron lung that takes me to a restaurant and orders liver and onions for me, I will junk that machine because I hate liver and onions. Like most people, I prefer to make my own decisions, and I'll be damned if I let anyone or anything deny me this defining aspect of my humanity" (37). Because of O'Brien's reliance on technology for survival, he recognizes that human interdependence on machines is already a fact of late-twentieth-century life, but he rejects the notion that humans must inevitably capitulate to machines.

Others respondents in the forum are less cautious. Marvin Minsky, one of the preeminent scientists working in AI, writes that "human beings are essentially machines." Even human consciousness, writes Minsky, "is just having certain kinds of short-term memory registers that describe a little bit about what you were recently thinking. In fact, consciousness in humans is not very strong." Minsky is enthusiastic about the extended life span, if not immortality, promised by fusion with computers: "If it was possible, I would have myself downloaded. Why not? The idea of not dying just after you've learned almost enough to solve a problem is compelling." He concludes that "evolution seems to be leading us to a machine consciousness" (37).

Author William Burroughs seems to agree with Minsky, predicting that human beings are nearing the end of the evolutionary line. Intervention is necessary, states Burroughs, to make "biologic alterations" and ensure the survival of the species in a reconfigured state. He draws a whimsical parallel between people who reject biological alteration in favor of retreating to "the simple American virtues" of "the church, the home, and the family" and dinosaurs who rejected mammalian crossbreeding in favor of growing bigger to ensure their survival (54).

Expressing himself in a somewhat more cautious vein than Minsky and Burroughs, cyberpunk author and critic Bruce Sterling writes that downloading human consciousness would be "socially disruptive" (50) and that what most people want is not bodiless immortality but to be "young and sexy and beautiful. For as long as posthumanly possible" (51). He predicts that most people will choose to retain their bodies but will obtain increasingly sophisticated technological enhancements to transform themselves radically. One respondent who expresses a willingness to go beyond technological augmentation is Mark Pauline, founder of Survival Research Laboratories and creator of awkward, gargantuan robotic machines that perform violent spectacles of destruction. Pauline writes that "my evolution, my life, is already determined by the multiplicity of possibilities of my connection with machines. If I could actually become a machine, I wouldn't; I would become machines, all machines" (40).

At issue in the debate is self-destruction, the annihilation of human beings. Moreover, the debate is taking place at a time when human bodies are already vulnerable to unprecedented threats of AIDS, cancer, nuclear annihilation, overpopulation, and environmental disasters. Devising plans to preserve human consciousness outside the body or to simulate human consciousness electronically indicates a desire to redefine the self in an age when the future of human existence is already precarious. The concept of simulated life indicates a desire to adapt for survival, but the process of adaptation in this case requires changing so drastically that survival has become indistinguishable from suicide.

Judging from the large quantity and popularity of texts concerned with posthuman life, the late twentieth century is marked by intense fascination with the idea of human obsolescence. This is, however, not a new phenomenon; interest in artificial human life extends back centuries, at least to ancient Greece. Ancient Greek myths and the sixteenth-century story of Joseph Golem, who was created from clay by an enterprising rabbi in Prague, are among the better-known tales about simulated life to have survived to the present day, but there have been many other such mythic tales, as well as actual attempts to simulate life over the course of the centuries. J. David Bolter writes that "there was perhaps never a moment in the ancient or modern history of Europe when no one was pursuing the idea of making a human being by other than the ordinary reproductive means."[20] The desire to simulate human life is thus deeply rooted in Western culture.

The craft of building humanoid automata flourished during the late seventeenth and eighteenth centuries, when the mechanistic worldview reigned. It reached its peak during the eighteenth century, when displays of automata were extremely popular, especially in the courts of European royalty, and Jacques de Vaucanson built his famous mechanical duck, which could eat, drink, flap its wings, and even excrete.[21] René Descartes himself had a female automaton named Francine. Psychologist Neil Frude writes:

We know very little about the characteristics of this figure, but it has been suggested that the mechanical doll often acted as a companion to the philosopher on his travels. When Francine was discovered on a sea voyage, hidden in a packing case, the ship's captain angrily threw "her" overboard. A bizarre twist is provided by the well-documented fact that Descartes had an illegitimate daughter from whom he was unhappily separated. Some authors have speculated that the figure was made to perfectly resemble this young woman, and it is certain that the daughter's name was Francine.[22]

Some things have clearly remained the same since the time when Descartes traveled with his artificial female companion; the male desire to construct an ideal woman by artificial means dates back at least to the ancient Greek myth of Pygmalion and Galatea and continues to this day in films (*Weird Science* [Hughes 1985], *Cherry 2000* [DeJarnatt 1988]) and on television (*Mann and Machine* [1992]).

The relationship between human beings and technology has changed dramatically since the seventeenth century, however, achieving an intimacy that was inconceivable until only recently. Human fusion with artificial devices has become a fact of life; prosthetic limbs and artificial organs are just two examples of how the human body incorporates technology's products. Researchers at Duke University are studying ways to use computer chips to restore vision to sightless human eyes.[23] By watching television and using computers we have all become dependent on the interface with electronic technology.

In fact, both scientific and popular culture texts extend the idea of this fusion much further. Hans Moravec envisions a way to make Descartes's metaphor of the mind divorced from the body literal by taking the human mind out of the brain. He describes how someday it will be possible for human mental functions to be surgically extracted from the human brain and transferred to computer software in a process he calls "transmigration." The useless human body with its brain tissue would then be discarded, while human consciousness would remain stored in computer terminals or, for the occasional outing, in mobile robots. He speculates briefly on the philosophical basis for his idea by contrasting two different positions toward the Cartesian question "what am I?" The first is the "body-identity position," which "assumes that a person is defined by the stuff of which a human body is made." The second, the "pattern-identity position," defines the essence of a person as the "pattern and the process going on in my head and body, not the machinery supporting the process." Moravec embraces the second, the pattern-identity position, explaining that "if the process is preserved, I am preserved. The rest is mere jelly."[24]

Despite the extreme nature of his ideas, Moravec is not an isolated mad scientist; he has had his vision of separating the human mind from the body endorsed by Marvin Minsky.[25] Both Moravec and Minsky deny that the postbiological future, whether populated by artificial intelligences, robots, or disembodied human minds, will be devoid of emotions, which have long been considered uniquely human attributes. Minsky rejects the Cartesian separation of reason from passion in his book about AI, *The Society of Mind*. He writes that whereas infants express emotional needs purely and spontaneously, adult emotions cannot be separated from learned intellectual behavior. He concludes that "beyond a certain point, to distinguish between the emotional and intellectual structures of an adult is merely to describe the same structures from different points of view."[26] Minsky's integration of human intellect and emotions evokes the theories of holistic medicine, but ironically, rather than attempt to preserve human life, Minsky's writings contemplate its extinction.

In the realm of fictional representation posthuman life has become commonplace, no longer requiring elaborate explanations but relying instead on cultural familiarity with the concept and imagery. In the highly profit-motivated Hollywood film industry, where sequels and spin-offs prevail, a successful film is often followed by a slew of others that recycle the imagery and narrative premise of the original. Constance Penley writes that the film *The Terminator* (Cameron 1984) "was quickly replicated by *Exterminator*, *Re-Animator*, *Eliminators*, *The Annihilators*, and the hardcore *The Sperminator*, all sound-alikes if not look-alikes."[27] Her list can be expanded to include the films *The Vindicator* and *The Russian Terminator*. There was also the inevitable sequel, *Terminator 2: Judgment Day*, as well as the comic book series *The Terminator*[28] and *RoboCop versus the Terminator*.[29] The Terminator texts join a huge number of other films, books, games, and comics based on the premise of a cyborg future. In the postmodern swirl of images and texts surrounding us, it is easy to encounter diverse and imaginative ways to represent posthuman life.

The Cartesian opposition between reason and emotion is apparent in many of pop culture's cyborg texts, typically equating machines with reason and humans with emotion in conventional fashion. An NBC television series that aired in the spring of 1992, *Mann and Machine*, which I analyze more fully in chapter 6, is based on the premise that its two cops, one human and the other a machine, represent two sharply contrasting modes: the machine is analytical, rational, and calm, whereas the human is emotional and intuitive. In the film *RoboCop* (Verhoeven 1987) the team of scientists who create RoboCop by fusing electronic elements with the remains of murdered police officer Alex J. Murphy design him to be a purely rational mechanical tool. Murphy's memories keep surfacing, however, as RoboCop seeks information about Murphy's wife and young son and about the vicious criminals who killed him. RoboCop has lost the ability fully to experience emotions, but he is stirred by the flickering remnants of feelings he can no longer understand. The Terminator, too, is designed for a single-minded, unemotional mission in the film *The Terminator* (Cameron 1984): to kill Sarah Connor. He has been programmed to terminate her, which is his only function, and the film follows his relentless pursuit of her.

Popular culture has pursued the implications of technological fusion most consistently in the subgenre of science fiction called cyberpunk, which began in the early 1980s. Cyberpunk combines an aggressive, anti-authoritarian punk sensibility rooted in urban street culture with a highly technological future where distinctions between technology and humanity have dissolved. As a unique exemplar of postmodernism, cyberpunk has been the subject of much critical attention. Three books in particular have elaborated intelligently on cyberpunk as postmodern: *Terminal Identity*, by Scott Bukatman, *Storming the Reality Studio*, edited by Larry McCaffery, and *Fiction 2000*, edited by George Slusser and Tom Shippey.[30]

In some respects cyberpunk revolves around a Cartesian separation of mind from body. When console cowboys jack into cyberspace in William Gibson's novels *Neuromancer, Count Zero*, and *Mona Lisa Overdrive*,[31] they leave their bodies behind to soar mentally through a "consensual hallucination" of three-dimensional data inside the computer matrix. They refer disparagingly to the bodies they have left behind as "meat." An early cyberpunk novel by Rudy Rucker entitled *Software*[32] presents perhaps the

FIG. 3. The Terminator on a relentless mission to kill
Sarah Connor in the film *The Terminator.*

closest popular-culture equivalent to Hans Moravec's transmigration scenario. In the novel an aging scientist living in retirement in Florida during the twenty-first century agrees to have his brain patterns transferred
out of his body by the superintelligent robots he created and set free during the twentieth century. The scientist is promised immortality and given
a robot body indistinguishable from his original organic body. After the
procedure, however, and much to his chagrin, he discovers that his brain
patterns are being stored in a computer hidden in a Mr. Frostee ice cream
truck controlled by the robots; consequently he does not have complete
control over himself.

Because Rucker's novel was published six years before Moravec's book,
it appears that the idea of extracting brain patterns originated in science
fiction. When asked by an interviewer how science fiction was important
in his development, Moravec indicated that it helped him to take his own
eccentric ideas seriously: "Otherwise you tend to think of local possibilities, within society as it exists, rather than thinking of radically different

things. It helped to keep getting the mind stretched at an early age."[33] Moravec's science, then, received validation from science fiction, a reversal of the traditional relationship between the two discourses. For this particular phenomenon, at least, the line between science and science fiction has become blurred. For some observers, this is part of a larger blurring between fact and fiction that characterizes our age. J. G. Ballard writes in his introduction to *Crash*:

I feel that the balance between fiction and reality has changed significantly in the past decade. Increasingly their roles are reversed. We live in a world ruled by fictions of every kind— mass merchandising, advertising, politics conducted as a branch of advertising, the instant translation of science and technology into popular imagery, the increasing blurring and intermingling of identities within the realm of consumer goods, the preempting of any free or original imaginative response to experience by the television screen. We live inside an enormous novel. For the writer in particular it is less and less necessary for him to invent the fictional content of his novel. The fiction is already there. The writer's task is to invent the reality.[34]

Along with the collapse between reality and fiction, the Cartesian mind/body duality is ultimately eclipsed by the concept of the cyborg. Rather than accomplish an ideal Enlightenment universe where human reason takes center stage, the cyborg undermines the very concept of "human." The cyborg's status is neither human nor artificial but a hybrid of the two, radically altering human subjectivity in the process. As feminist theorist and historian of science Donna Haraway writes in her "Manifesto for Cyborgs," a human-centered universe rests on a system of dualities:

real/artificial, natural/cultural, male/female, young/old, analytical/emotional, past/present, and alive/dead, as well as human/technological.[35] When the boundary between human and artificial collapses, all of the other dualities also dissolve, and their two parts become indistinguishable, displacing humans from the unique and privileged position they maintained in Enlightenment philosophy. Transgressed boundaries, in fact, are a central feature of postmodernism, and the cyborg is the ultimate transgressed boundary. Fredric Jameson goes so far as to identify cyberpunk fiction as "the supreme literary expression if not of postmodernism, then of late capitalism itself."[36]

Cyberpunk renders uncertain any basis for an authentic human identity. Technology allows cyberpunk characters to alter themselves in any way they choose, abandoning any semblance of their original identities. In some cyberpunk texts characters change their identities the way most people change socks. Their identities, moreover, are often technological constructs without origin in human consciousness. In George Alec Effinger's trilogy, *When Gravity Fails, A Fire in the Sun,* and *The Exile Kiss,*[37] characters load software directly into their electronically wired brains. They "chip in" personality modules called "moddies" and "add-on chips" called "daddies" sold in "modshops" where the biggest sellers are sex, drugs, and religious ecstasy. Some of the characters have long ago relinquished any authentic personality by constantly relying on moddies and daddies. Laila, who owns a modshop, has a different identity chipped in every time she appears, becoming, among others, a film star and a fictional character named "Emma: Madame Bovary: Dentist of Tomorrow."[38]

What results is the world of simulations theorized by Jean Baudrillard, a hyperreality where "it is no longer a question of imitation, nor of reduplication, nor even of parody. It is rather a question of substituting signs of the real for the real itself."[39] A commercial for Sony televisions in our own time, not in a cyberpunk future, succinctly illustrates Baudrillard's observation when it shows a family standing on the rim of the Grand Canyon, admiring its beauty; instead of seeing the spectacular view itself, however, they look at the vista on a television perched on the canyon's rim. The

"Grand Canyon" on television *is* the Grand Canyon for this family and, by extension, for everyone watching the commercial on their own televisions. The "real" has been displaced by layer on layer of images.

The cyberpunk movement was influenced in its depiction of the late-twentieth-century rift between reality and appearances by a classic science-fiction novella titled *The Girl Who Was Plugged In*, published in 1973 by James Tiptree Jr. (a pseudonym for Alice B. Sheldon).[40] In the novella a beautiful, vibrant young woman named Delphi, who achieves fame and fortune as a media celebrity and product promoter, is actually a remotely controlled hollow shell operated by a hideous, disfigured young woman named P. Burke, who is kept in an underground cabinet. P. Burke has become the tool of advertisers who exploit her despair in an age when advertising has become illegal. Her only desire is to be the lovely Delphi, just as members of the viewing audience figuratively lose their identities when, hoping to capture a small part of Delphi's beauty and luxuriant lifestyle, they are cajoled into buying the products she promotes. Now, over twenty years after the publication of *The Girl Who Was Plugged In*, body-altering procedures are becoming as elaborate as their fictional counterparts; it is already possible to create permanent makeup by using a tattoo gun to inject pigment under the skin.[41]

Minds and bodies change like chameleons in cyberpunk, going beyond the merely fragmented subjectivity found in other postmodern texts to display complete instability. Even when they present human consciousness as preserved through fusion with electronic devices, cyberpunk texts question whether the fused consciousness can still be called human. In William Gibson's novel *Count Zero* an immensely wealthy man named Josef Virek, whose dying body has been confined to a vat in a suburb outside Stockholm for over a decade, creates computer-synthesized constructs of himself inhabiting synthesized spaces—virtual realities—that are exact duplicates of real spaces. Although Virek's body and his environment are both artificial constructs, they have complete three-dimensional verisimilitude for "real" human beings who are transported to the environments to meet with Virek. It can be argued that Virek main-

tains his human existence because his consciousness controls the illusions, but another character in the novel calls him "far from human."[42]
Virek's consciousness, after all, has become only one component in a
much larger technological system.

One of the alterable characteristics in cyberpunk is sexual identity.
Technology provides cyberpunk characters freedom from their biological
sex, rendering the opposition between real and artificial thoroughly ambiguous. In Walter Jon Williams's novel *Hardwired*, a lovely and innocent-looking twenty-year-old blond woman is actually an eighty-year-old
rich Russian man who has transferred his personality into a new body.[43]
In Effinger's trilogy, moreover, female characters are sometimes not really women but surgically altered "sexchanges," like today's transsexuals.[44]
In these examples, however, characters who change their sexual identity
are still subject to traditional cultural norms; they have changed their
bodies, but the societies around them continue to treat men and women
according to patriarchal dictates. Characters can choose to become male
or female, but they still function within a patriarchal system that elevates
men's interests above women's.

In some cyberpunk texts human beings have become extinct, and the
universe is populated by a variety of posthuman species. Bruce Sterling's
Shaper/Mechanist series, consisting of five short stories and a novel, follows the struggle between two adversarial posthuman species, the Shapers
and the Mechanists, for control of the solar system.[45] Not only are humans obsolete in the series, but Earth has been displaced in the planetary
hierarchy by other, more important planets. Humans are a distant memory
in Sterling's future, and Earth is merely the last remnant of a long-
vanished era. A vestige of human philosophy exists in the two warring
species, however: the Shaper/Mechanist opposition evokes the Cartesian
mind/body duality. The conflict is between the Shapers, who use genetic
engineering to design their organic bodies and extend their lives, and the
Mechanists, who have become increasingly mechanical as they incorporate technology into their cyborg bodies.

But even the Shaper/Mechanist conflict is being superseded in Sterling's future, where new, alien ideologies bearing no relationship to the Cartesian worldview are gaining dominance, eliminating the final traces of a human point of view. Species that flourish are those that have adopted a hive mentality patterned after insect societies; individual life has no value apart from its function to prolong the survival of the species. Like the postorganic Borg in the television series *Star Trek: The Next Generation*, Sterling's hive societies rapaciously absorb any other species they encounter, integrating new knowledge and skills into the collective consciousness.

One human trait that persists in Sterling's Shaper/Mechanist series is greed, particularly in a powerful alien species called the Investors. In the story "Twenty Evocations," when the Shaper Nikolai tells an Investor that he is "interested in alien philosophies . . . the answers of other species to the great questions of existence," the reptilian Investor responds, "But there is only one central question. . . . We have pursued its answer from star to star. We were hoping that you would help us answer it." The one central question posed by the Investor is "What is it you have that we want?"[46] The Investor's elevation of greed to a philosophy of life illustrates the destructive aspects of the Enlightenment belief in progress, for it has justified horrific abuses in the name of advancement.

Along with relinquishing a firm definition of human existence, cyberpunk and most cyborg imagery also relinquish the belief that the future holds the promise of a better world. Cyberpunk futures are inevitably dystopian; the environment has been ravaged beyond repair, and the entire solar system is controlled by extraordinarily wealthy corporations, while most people live in abject poverty. Humans have plundered the Earth and instituted a capitalist aristocracy. Individual rights are virtually nonexistent; people must fend for themselves in a hostile environment. Instead of offering the promise of progress, as it did for Enlightenment thinkers during the Industrial Revolution, technology is used by the wealthy elite to expand their powers and by the underclass to survive and escape into fantasy.

People have always been influenced by prevailing philosophies and ideologies when contemplating their relationship to technology. In fact, philosophy and technology have always maintained a close connection. J. David Bolter's book *Turing's Man* is based on the premise that

> *technology is as much a part of classical and*
> *Western culture as philosophy and science and*
> *that these "high" and "lowly" expressions of*
> *culture are closely related. It makes sense to*
> *examine Plato and pottery together in order to*
> *understand the Greek world, Descartes and the*
> *mechanical clock together to understand Europe*
> *in the seventeenth and eighteenth centuries. In*
> *the same way, it makes sense to regard the*
> *computer as a technological paradigm for the*
> *science, philosophy, even the art of the coming*
> *generation.*[47]

Bolter uses the term "defining technologies" to designate devices or crafts that have been particularly influential because they have provided powerful metaphors for an era.[48] In the seventeenth century Descartes and Leibniz, among others, used the clock metaphor to explain the workings of the natural world. Hence, animals were described as being like clockwork mechanisms. Human bodies, too, operate according to mechanical principles in the Cartesian system, as Descartes explains in his sixth meditation:

> *A clock, composed of wheels and counterweights,*
> *is no less exactly obeying all the laws of nature*
> *when it is badly made and does not mark the*
> *time correctly than when it completely fulfills the*
> *intention of its maker; so also the human body*
> *may be considered as a machine, so built and*
> *composed of bones, nerves, muscles, veins, blood,*
> *and skin that even if there were no mind in it, it*
> *would not cease to move in all the ways that it*

does at present when it is not moved under the
direction of the will, nor consequently with the
aid of the mind.[49]

What separates human beings from animals and machines, according to Descartes, is the human's nonmechanical mind, which is animated by the soul and capable of speech and reason.[50] Although Descartes excluded the human mind from his mechanistic worldview, some later thinkers made no such distinctions. During the eighteenth century the French physician Julien Offray de la Mettrie declared, "Let us conclude bravely that man is a machine" and consequently was forced to spend the rest of his life in exile from France.[51] In our own century Marvin Minsky is well known for his statement that "the brain happens to be a meat machine."[52]

Machines have undergone immense changes during the course of the twentieth century. Mechanical technology, with its engines, gears, pistons, and shafts, has been joined and in many ways superseded by the increasingly miniaturized microcircuitry of electronic technology. As machines have changed, so has culture, each one shaping the other in a tight web of influence. J. David Bolter suggests this line of influence when he identifies the computer as our culture's dominant technological paradigm. Bolter argues that the computer, as the defining technology of the late twentieth century, has influenced the way we think about ourselves. It reinforces the notion that human beings are purely cerebral entities capable of being simulated by artificial intelligence or absorbed into technology. From this perspective the computer is a culmination of Descartes's celebration of the disembodied human mind.

As contemporary cultural theorists have pointed out, the computer is also a uniquely postmodern technology. Postmodernism, the dominant ethos of the late twentieth century, has been identified by Fredric Jameson, among others, as starting in the immediate post–World War II years, when multinational corporations began to control the world's economic and cultural systems and the driving force behind social organization became the perpetual consumption of goods. Although there is no consensus on how to define postmodernism, there are a number of compelling descriptions, among them Jameson's, that help to explain our late-twentieth-century social reality.[53]

Postmodern consumer society is an all-encompassing marketplace of products; everything in it has been commodified, and it surrounds us with advertising, packaged images, and ever-changing fashions in clothes, music, and "life-styles." Images and sounds bombard postmodern humans and create a phantasmagoria of idealized human bodies. The endless depictions of human bodies have in effect replaced actual human bodies in the public imagination, and it can thus be argued, as do postmodern cultural critics Arthur and Marilouise Kroker, that the human body is already obsolete. They ask, "why the concern over the body today if not to emphasize the fact that the (natural) body in the postmodern condition has *already* disappeared, and what we experience as the body is only a fantastic simulacra of body rhetorics?" The physical body, argue the Krokers, has become obscured by the body rhetorics of advertising, economics, politics, psychoanalysis, science, and sports. Not just the physical body but also the discursive body has disappeared into what the Krokers call "panic bodies: an inscribed surface onto which are projected all the grisly symptoms of culture burnout." Panic bodies, in the Krokers' description, are "incited less by the languages of accumulation than fascinating, because catastrophic, signs of self-[extermination], self-liquidation, and self-cancellation."[54] According to the Krokers, bodies have become expendable in the late twentieth century as the economy collapses and the culture implodes.

Even our experience of space and time, argues Jameson, has been transformed under postmodernism. Time has collapsed into a perpetual present, in which everything from the past has been severed from its historical context in order to circulate anew in the present, devoid of its original meanings but contributing to the cluttered texture of our commodified surroundings. The result, he writes, is historical amnesia, a lack of knowledge about the past that, in its pathological form, resembles the schizophrenic's inability to remember anything and consequent inability to sustain a coherent identity.

William Gibson comments on the trivialization of history in *Virtual Light*. In this novel, which is set in the near future, an elderly man named Skinner observes the incoherent society around him with both cynicism and compassion. Skinner, writes Gibson, "had this thing about history. How it was turning into plastic."[55] In his society, as in ours, the past is perceived as an array of knickknacks. Skinner understands this literally as well as figuratively, for he ekes out a living by selling things, many of them quite useless, that he has accumulated over the course of his life.

Jameson characterizes postmodern space as bewildering and disorienting, crowded by a pastiche of disconnected artifacts and seemingly designed for a nonhuman species with a more advanced sensual apparatus. In Jameson's example, the Bonaventure Hotel in Los Angeles, it is difficult to locate the entrance, much less get one's bearings inside the lobby's confusing layout. Jameson identifies this bewildering use of space as the postmodern architectural equivalent to the logic of multinational capitalism, in which any attempt to identify precisely where corporate control resides is mystified by a labyrinthine tangle of subsidiaries and interlocking networks.[56]

Postmodernism, then, is already in some ways a posthuman system beyond human sensory capacities. William Gibson has said that we are already in a posthuman age.[57] With our dependence on technology and the availability of artificial body parts, humans have already developed into hybrid creatures. Additionally, the logic of multinational capitalism is one that favors a few wealthy individuals—the sort of people who, in Gibson's fiction, have become something other than human as a result of their immense riches and their absolute lack of scruples. In Gibson's universe the rich elite prosper at the expense of their humanity, while the poor are crushed by a system that does not care whether they live or die or whether there is anything of value in human existence.

What Gibson makes clear is that when human life is perceived as expendable, as in Hans Moravec's speculations, it is the disfranchised and impoverished who are at risk. In a highly stratified late-capitalist society, not all human life is treated equally. The concept of obsolescence for humans becomes in practice a form of social Darwinism: the survival of

those who have the economic means to finance their continued existence. In fact, in Gibson's and other cyberpunk novels wealthy individuals
spend fortunes to extend their lives beyond their biological limits. Josef
Virek in Gibson's *Count Zero* monomaniacally spends inconceivable
amounts of money in an attempt to attain immortality. In *Neuromancer*
Gibson describes a shady businessperson named Julius Deane as being
"one hundred and thirty-five years old, his metabolism assiduously warped
by a weekly fortune in serums and hormones. His primary hedge against
aging was a yearly pilgrimage to Tokyo, where genetic surgeons re-set the
code of his DNA."[58] In the same novel the patriarch of the Tessier-Ashpool
family has had himself cryogenically frozen along with his descendants,
who have also been cloned into multiple copies. The family members take
turns thawing and ruling their vast empire. In George Alec Effinger's trilogy Friedlander Bey, an extremely wealthy crime lord, is "about two hundred years old, but he'd had a lot of body modifications and transplants."[59]

Since wealth allows certain individuals to prolong their lives artificially
in these novels, human obsolescence is confined to the poor. As Gibson
makes clear in *Virtual Light*, by the year 2005, just a short leap into the
future, the middle class will have disappeared, leaving only the very rich
and the very poor. In this novel Sammy Sal, a tough black bicycle messenger, explains to another messenger that there used to be a middle class,
but now there is "only but two kinds of people." He continues, "But what
happens on the interface? What happens when we touch?" and then responds that the only contact between rich and poor revolves around crime,
sex, and drugs.[60]

The superrich are like a separate species; they dally with the poor and
treat them with contempt. This is apparent as well in George Alec Effinger's
trilogy, where the quest for immortality has created a black market in
human organs, and the poor are murdered for their body parts. In Effinger's
novel *A Fire in the Sun* two powerful crime lords who compete in most
matters have cooperated in one area: they maintain a "Phoenix File," a
list of names of subordinates who are in line to be killed for their organs.
As one of the crime lords explains, "The Phoenix File is life to me."[61] In

this highly hierarchical social structure, it is a luxury to speak of human obsolescence, for it is always someone else who risks becoming obsolete. While the life span of the rich lengthens through artificial enhancement, that of the poor dwindles.

In the inhospitable clutter of commodified postmodern space, human perception is invited to skim the surface rather than explore meaningful depths. This postmodern depthlessness is exemplified by the flatness of the television and computer screens that pervade our lives and encourage a flattening of all perceptual experiences. Jean Baudrillard explains how postmodern computerized existence differs in fundamental ways from earlier experience.

We used to live in the imaginary world of the mirror, of the divided self and of the stage, of otherness and alienation. Today we live in the imaginary world of the screen, of the interface and the reduplication of contiguity and networks. All our machines are screens. We too have become screens, and the interactivity of men has become the interactivity of screens. Nothing that appears on the screen is meant to be deciphered in depth, but actually to be explored instantaneously, in an abreaction immediate to meaning—or an immediate convolution of the poles of representation.[62]

Baudrillard asserts that the psychological depth explored and analyzed by Freud in the late nineteenth and early twentieth centuries no longer characterizes late-twentieth-century human beings. Postmodern humans experience themselves as surface phenomena without depth and experience their interactions with each other as occurring without distance, as if all life were reduced to immediacy and the flat surface of the computer or television screen. Film scholar Scott Bukatman has identified the new state of human existence as "terminal identity" in his book of that title.[63] His term simultaneously captures the integration of humans with computers and the cessation of human life as we know it. In addition Vivian Sobchack, in her book on American science-fiction films, explains that "only superficial beings without 'psyche,' without depth, can successfully maneuver a space that exists solely to display."[64] She expands on the new depthlessness of lived experience:

> As a function of this new "sense" of space, our
> depth perception has become less dominant as a
> mode of representing and dealing with the world.
> To a great degree, it has become flattened by the
> superficial electronic "dimensionality" of
> movement experience as occurring on—not in—
> the screens of computer terminals, video games,
> music videos, and movies. . . . Our experience of
> spatial contiguity has also been radically altered
> by digital representation. Fragmented into
> discrete and contained units by both microchips
> and strobe lights, space has lost much of its
> contextual function as the ground for the
> continuities of time, movement, and event. Space
> is now more often a "text" than a "context."[65]

The development and dispersion of computers coincided with the post–World War II rise of postmodernism. According to Tom Forester in his book *High-Tech Society*, the "microelectronics revolution" started around 1946, at about the same time that the massive ENIAC (Electronic Numerical Integrator and Calculator), the first general-purpose electronic digital computer, was introduced at the University of Pennsylvania.[66] Although he omits the context of postmodernism, Forester characterizes computer technology's impact on society as revolutionary, especially with the dispersion of personal computers. Forester writes, "The nations of the world are caught up in a revolution: a technological revolution, which is bringing about dramatic changes in the way we live and work—and maybe even think." He calls microelectronics "the most remarkable technology ever to confront mankind."[67]

The computer has had many dramatic influences on our lives, including helping to make information a highly valued commodity, and powerful organizations have access to the greatest quantities of information. Wealthy corporations and well-entrenched government agencies have the means to acquire the most expensive technology and amass the most information, which leaves others disfranchised, outside the network of knowledge. There are, however, other ways to imagine computers fitting into society, ways that encourage equal access to data rather than strengthen existing hierarchies of power. Jean-François Lyotard ends *The Postmodern Condition* by contrasting two scenarios for computerization:

We are finally in a position to understand how the computerization of society affects this problematic. It could become the "dream" instrument for controlling and regulating the market system, extended to include knowledge itself and governed exclusively by the performativity principle. In that case, it would inevitably involve the use of terror. But it could also aid groups discussing metaprescriptives by supplying them with the information they usually lack for making knowledgeable decisions. The line to follow for computerization to take the second of these two paths is, in principle, quite simple: give the public free access to the memory and data banks.[68]

Lyotard writes that the second scenario would "respect both the desire for justice and the desire for the unknown," a combination that maintains a commitment to social equality without succumbing, as is often the case, to technophobia.

Using a similar formulation Manuel De Landa, in his book *War in the Age of Intelligent Machines*, carefully documents the history of technology used for warfare, including ENIAC and other early computers, and shows how the latest phase, the "predatory computer," will make possible "autonomous weapons systems capable of fighting wars entirely on their own."[69] De Landa argues that the U.S. military has grown to enormous proportions and has infiltrated society so fully that the line between civilian and military endeavors has become blurred. The history of computer development provides the best example of the blurred boundary between military and civilian; industries, universities, and the Pentagon have collaborated closely on computer design and applications. Even so, concludes De Landa, military hegemony over computers is not the only option for the future. He cites the independent computer work done by "hackers and fringe scientists" who developed "interactivity in order to put computer power in everybody's hands." Their contribution, writes De Landa, is "just one more instance of the fact that the forces of technology are not easy for institutions to capture and enslave."[70] For Lyotard and De Landa, the opportunity remains for computerized societies to avoid authoritarian models and instead make the computerized circulation of information part of egalitarian communities.

Computers, according to Lyotard, are a recent component of a larger cultural transformation that has taken place over the course of the nineteenth and twentieth centuries: the "delegitimation" of scientific knowledge, a rejection of scientific metanarratives. By the late twentieth century faith has eroded in the notion that science can provide pure, objective, totalizing truth that extends beyond the borders of its own terms to encompass all of reality. Lyotard writes that "the grand narrative has lost its credibility" and that "it is recognized that the conditions of truth, in other words, the rules of the game of science, are immanent in that game, that they can only be established within the bonds of a debate that is already scientific in nature, and that there is no other proof that the rules are good than the consensus extended to them by the experts." "Consensus," he asserts, "has become an outmoded and suspect value."[71]

Lyotard's position has been criticized for its contradictions and its idealism. N. Katherine Hayles points out that Lyotard constructs his own narrative to explain historical developments while at the same time rejecting the notion of narrative accuracy. She further chides him for idealistically believing that small-scale local knowledge can compete successfully against corporations with global control over the use of computer technologies, for computers, like all technologies, "will be embedded in the same institutions that have brought us to this critical point."[72]

The most thorough critique of scientific claims of objectivity has come from feminists, for whom the history of science is fraught with patriarchal ideological assumptions put forth in the guise of dispassionate truth. Not only have women's bodies been the terrain of scientific scrutiny, but scientific language has often relied on gendered metaphors that give patriarchal ideas about gender difference the aura of absolute truth. Instead of existing in isolation, science has participated in a network of ideologies that uphold patriarchal institutions. According to philosopher Sandra Harding, "Ideologies of gender enter into the most unlikely realms of scientific inquiry, informing and shaping the perception of scientists and even the direction of experimentation (not to mention public reaction). But we also find, conversely, that scientific representations of the feminine body are themselves a constitutive part of wider social discourses that are informed and shaped in their turn by economic, class, and racial ideologies."[73] In her book *Whose Science? Whose Knowledge?* she continues, "the sciences are part and parcel, woof and warp, of the social orders from which they emerge and which support them." She cautions that "it is important to see that the focus should not be on whether individuals in the history of science were sexist" but rather on how scientific ideas have functioned as a component of larger cultural meanings and how those meanings are not value neutral but often uphold dominant patriarchal views.[74]

Among the most carefully researched analyses of how scientific knowledge has complemented both patriarchal and racist ideologies is Donna Haraway's study of the history of primatology, *Primate Visions*.[75] Traditional primate studies, she shows, have revolved around the binary terms nature/culture and sex/gender and under the guise of objective science have expressed value judgments used to explain human as well as animal behavior. Thus, primatology has been used to justify cultural constructions of gender by attempting to locate their origins in nature and in biological sex. Hardly disinterested observers, primatologists have fortified ideas already prevalent in their cultures about what constitutes "natural" behavior for men and women.

Not only the discourses of science but also those of technology have been analyzed by feminist scholars. *Machina Ex Dea*, edited by Joan Rothschild, is a collection of essays that examines how histories of technology have excluded women and how women have contributed to technological developments.[76] In *Teaching Technology from a Feminist Perspective* Rothschild describes some of the central issues involved in feminist reexaminations of technological history and outlines a series of courses designed to teach students about the connections between gender and technology.[77]

The feminist analysis of scientific discourses is one aspect of a much larger cultural crisis over issues of gender and sexuality. Late-twentieth-century Western culture is divided more than ever before between those who reject and those who cling to the patriarchal assumption of male superiority. Much of the debate over gender roles is taking place overtly in politics, the legal system, and the public statements of proponents for both sides. There are also more subtle ways that the crisis over gender and sexuality informs the contemporary scene, however. In the arena of fictional representation the imagery of human fusion with artificial components is replete with metaphors pertaining to sex and gender. Representations of technology have long been gendered and eroticized, so this is not a new phenomenon, but an analysis of recent imagery reveals the particular desires and fears of the late twentieth century, a time when the future of human beings in any form, male or female, can no longer be taken for granted.

In the debate over gender roles, both sides have implicitly turned to the legacy of Descartes to justify their positions. The patriarchal system, with its rigid gender categories, has relied on the mind/body duality to relegate women to childbearing and domestic roles by defining a woman's identity on the basis of her reproductive organs. Additionally, patriarchy has used the duality to associate masculinity with the rational life of the mind and therefore with all things cultural and technological. Women are identified with the body's irrational drives and the so-called natural world. Thus, the idea of male superiority rests on a system of dualities.

One aspect of feminism, then, has been to reject the patriarchal system of dualities. Nonetheless, poststructuralist feminism implicitly draws on the mind/body duality to argue that gender roles are constructed by culture, not biologically determined. It is not anatomical difference but language, family, and social institutions that construct subjectivity. This view, ironically, is similar to Hans Moravec's pattern-identity position. It releases women—and for that matter, men—from identities based on bodily functions. It also allows theorists such as Donna Haraway, Avital Ronell, and Valie Export to articulate nontechnophobic feminist positions.[78] After all, it may be too late to reject the cyborg existence. We are all already jacked in.

CHAPTER 2

The Pleasure of the Interface

Sex times technology equals the future.

J. G. Ballard[1]

POPULAR CULTURE has embraced the idea of artificial sexuality. In pop culture human fusion with computer technology is often represented in positive terms, creating a hybrid computer-human that displays highly evolved intelligence and escapes the imperfections of the human body. Nevertheless, while disparaging the imperfect human body, pop culture simultaneously uses language and imagery associated with the body and bodily functions to represent its vision of human/technological perfection. Computer technologies thus occupy a contradictory discursive position, representing both escape from the physical body and fulfillment of erotic desire. To quote science-fiction author J. G. Ballard again,

I believe that organic sex, body against body, skin area against skin area, is becoming no longer possible. . . . What we're getting is a whole new order of sexual fantasies, involving a different order of experiences, like car crashes, like traveling in jet aircraft, the whole overlay of new technologies, architecture, interior design, communications, transport, merchandising. These things are beginning to reach into our lives and change the interior design of our sexual fantasies.[2]

Popular culture often intensifies corporeality in its representation of cyborgs. A mostly electronic system is represented as its other: a muscular human body with robotic parts that heighten physicality and sexuality. In other words, many contemporary texts represent a future where human bodies are on the verge of becoming obsolete but sexuality nevertheless prevails.

Sex is not a newcomer to science and technology, as feminist scholars have made clear in their analyses of scientific discourses. An example of sex in a description of technology can be found in a 1968 issue of the journal *Technology and Culture*, where author Lee Hart is quoted as writing that "machines may well have erotic fantasies when the machine 'perceives' the rising nipple of a well-turned dial."[3] Thrusting and pumping industrial machines have long evoked sexual imagery for human observers, but Hart suggests that the machines themselves are motivated by sexual desire and erotic fantasies. Sex, it seems, monopolizes the thoughts not only of human scholars in the field of technology but also of the machines they study.

Computer discourses are products of their cultures and are infused with cultural assumptions about gender and sexuality. A staid computer magazine, *International Spectrum*, subtitled *The Businessperson's Com-*

puter *Magazine*, has inside the front cover of its November/December 1989 issue an advertisement for Sequoia hardware that shows a tape measure marked in intervals not of inches but of numbers of hardware users, accompanied by the question, "Can your Pick hardware measure up to this?" (Pick is a business-oriented office operating system.) Its association of computer hardware with penis length assumes a male consumer and makes explicit the conjunction of sexuality and technology that pervades computer discourses.

There seems to be an irresistible compulsion to associate computers and the computer world with sexuality. Jack Rochester and John Gantz, for example, start their book *The Naked Computer* with an introduction titled "The Mating Call," in which they inform the reader, "You're in love. You just don't know it yet. . . . But you might as well join the orgy, succumb to the pleasures of the information age. After all, a computer has already changed your life."[4] The magazine *Future Sex* examines how technology can facilitate sexuality and features high-tech sex toys in photographs, drawings, essays, and stories. A sexy discourse also surrounds computer technology in the hip cyberpunk journal *Mondo 2000*. Its editorial staff list includes the position of Domineditrix, and issue number 1 displays "micro chic: artificial intelligence to wear," with a model posing provocatively wearing electronic circuitry that has been assembled into breastplates.[5] Issue number 5 includes photographs of nude women with elaborate contraptions made of electronic circuitry strapped to their crotches, breasts, and buttocks. They are described in the accompanying text as maenads (women who participated in Dionysian rites), and a poem printed alongside them includes the following lurid lines:

Groaning, moaning, on your knees
panther, Niger, come to me
blood and milk together feed the pleasure

carmine, throbbing, senses reel
fleshy mystery, pagan meal
Dionysus screams as we give pleasure.[6]

Cybersex has become a marketing gimmick, lending an aura of novelty to otherwise conventional products. For example, the compact disc (CD) titled *Cyborgasm* promises "the wildest erotic experience of your life" on its cover, but the contents fail to justify the title. Sixteen cuts recorded in "3-D audio" provide monologues and dialogues involving a variety of sexual encounters and fantasies. Susie Bright, for example, speaks the part of a masochistic love-slave kept in a cage. As Chris Hudak puts it bluntly in his review, "*there is nothing remotely 'cyber' about any of this. It's a fucking CD. Literally.*" Hudak speculates that the makers of the *Cyborgasm* CD and others capitalizing on the trend "slap the word 'cyber' somewhere on it, and PHHHHBBBTTTHAHAHAHA, all the way to the bank."[7] Joining the parade to the bank are the creators of the book *The Joy of Cybersex: An Underground Guide to Electronic Erotica*, published in 1993. The book's authors describe erotic software and state-of-the-art technology, interview people working in the computer sex industry, and provide an erotic program on a computer disk.[8]

For the computer user, sex software has been around for years and continues to sell well. There is a wide selection of floppy disks available showing provocative shots of nude models ("Take a good hard look at Cindy with her 5 hottest poses").[9] Erotic films have been transferred from video-disc to CD-ROM (compact disc–read only memory). Interactive CD-ROMs and diskettes give users a chance to choose their thrills. For example, a CD-ROM advertisement touts its product thus: "Join the voluptuous guard as she spies on the tenants of a luxurious beach front resort. You will be amazed at the activity that goes on around this compound. And when the supervisor catches her, you decide the 'punishment.'"[10] An early program named "Whorehouse" has the players vie to become "King Pimp"; "play begins by putting your wife on the sidewalk."[11] Currently, Mike Saenz, the creator of the interactive programs "MacPlaymates" and "Virtual Valerie," cannot keep up with the high demand for his products.[12]

"Virtual Valerie," one of the best-selling CD-ROM programs, reveals what is implicit in all erotic computer software: technology, not physical sex, is the true locus of computerized sexuality. "Virtual Valerie: Director's Cut" invites the player to enter Valerie's high-rise apartment building, ride the elevator to her third-floor apartment, and explore her apartment before finally ending up on the sofa for foreplay with Valerie. Lavish attention is paid to the gadgets in the building: with a click of the mouse the elevator doors slide open and closed with a sensual hiss, Valerie's telephone dials several numbers, her toilet flushes, her shower drips and sprays water, her refrigerator opens, her garbage disposal grinds, and her entertainment center screens demo versions of CD-ROM games, among other effects. One player reports that he and his friends "had more fun blowing up the microwave than getting Valerie off." Even the paintings on Valerie's walls come to life: one shows King Kong surrounded by buzzing airplanes against the New York skyline, and another one shows cars falling off a conveyor belt into a funnel with a "destroy" switch and then falling onto another conveyor belt and moving on. Everywhere throughout Valerie's apartment building, technology promises fun and excitement. Not surprisingly, sex with Valerie turns out to be mechanical as well. She remains in one position—on all fours—as a dildo enters her from behind. The player moves the mouse back and forth quickly to operate the dildo, and a meter registers intensity levels until Valerie says "I'm coming" and vibrates. The game is over. Valerie's mechanical charms join those of the kitchen sink, dishwasher, and microwave, lying dormant until the next time they are called on to play.

Mike Saenz admits in an interview about his "Virtual Valerie" program that "the sex bits could be better." He explains, "Valerie's world is so detailed that it became this huge project, and by the time I got to the sex, I was, you might say, fucked out. We've had complaints that people are getting Carpal Tunnel Syndrome from trying to please Valerie."[13] Perhaps the sex bits could be better, but Saenz succeeded in making Valerie's apartment a postmodern techno-erotic playground.

For a more fully interactive experience, computer networks with names such as "Throbnet," "Sleazenet," and "After Dark" have made it possible for people to communicate at length with each other about sex with complete anonymity. One account describes the situation as follows: "Pioneered by computer hobbyists, the exchange of explicit and personal sexual material via personal computer and phone lines has taken on international proportions in the last three years."[14] The cover story of the April 1993 issue of *NewMedia*, a magazine covering "multimedia technologies for desktop computer users," is about "digital sex" and reports on ways that computers are being used for sexual purposes. The article reports that "dozens of private bulletin boards that specialize in adult chat areas and graphics exchange have sprung up. The largest—Event Horizons— raked in $3 million last year and boasts 64 lines and a clientele of 35,000 customers internationally." The editor and publisher of *Boardwatch* magazine is quoted as saying that the alt.sex newsgroups on the Internet are "definitely among the higher traffic areas."[15] Computers have seduced some users away from face-to-face romantic interactions altogether. As cultural critic Mark Dery writes regarding the phenomenon he calls "mechano-eroticism," "The only thing better than making love *like* a machine, it seems, is making love *with* a machine."[16]

The pop-culture discourse on computers reveals a new manifestation of the simultaneous revulsion and fascination with the human body that has existed throughout the Western cultural tradition. Ambivalence toward the body has traditionally been played out most explicitly in texts labeled pornographic, where the construction of desire often depends on an element of aversion. That which has been prohibited by censorship, for example, frequently becomes highly desirable. It was only in the nineteenth century, however, that pornography was introduced as a concept and a word, although its etymology dates back to the Greek *pornographos*, "writing about prostitutes." Walter Kendrick argues in his book *The Secret Museum* that the signifier "pornography" has never had a specific signified but constitutes a shifting ideological framework that has been imposed on a variety of texts since its inception.[17] During the late twentieth century sexual representation has crossed boundaries that previously separated the organic from the technological. This phenomenon is just part of the new permeability of the boundary separating machines from organisms. As Donna Haraway writes, "Late twentieth-century machines have made thoroughly ambiguous the difference between natural and arti-

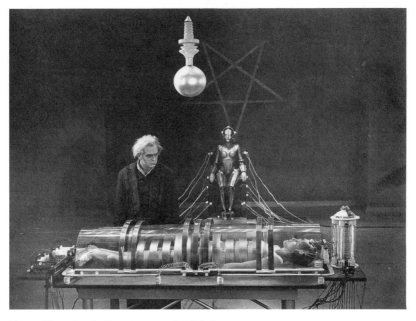

Fig. 4. The scientist Rotwang transfers life from a
human woman, Maria, to his female robot in the film
Metropolis.

ficial, mind and body, self-developing and externally designed, and many
other distinctions that used to apply to organisms and machines. Our machines are disturbingly lively, and we ourselves frighteningly inert."[18]

Sexual images of technology are by no means new; modernist texts in
the early twentieth century frequently eroticized technology. The film
Metropolis is a classic example of the early-twentieth-century fascination
with technology. It combines celebration of technological efficiency with
fear of technology's power to destroy humanity by running out of control.
The film expresses this dual response in sexual terms: a robot shaped like
a woman represents technology's simultaneous allure and powerful threat.
The robot is distinguished by its overt sexuality, for it is its seductive manner that triggers a chaotic worker revolt. As Andreas Huyssen argues in his
essay "The Vamp and the Machine," modernist texts tend to equate machines with women, displacing and projecting fears of overpowering technology onto patriarchal fears of female sexuality.[19] Huyssen writes that

technology was not always linked to female sexuality; the two became associated after the beginning of the nineteenth century, just as machines came to be perceived as threatening entities capable of vast, uncontrollable destruction. In nineteenth-century literature human life often appears to be vulnerable to the massive destructive potential of machines. Earlier, in the eighteenth century, before the Industrial Revolution installed machinery in the workplace on a grand scale, mechanization offered merely a playful diversion in the form of the mechanical automata, designed to look male as often as female, that achieved great popularity in the European cities where they were displayed.

Cyborgs, however, belong to the information age, when, as K. C. D'Alessandro writes, "huge, thrusting machines have been replaced with the circuitry maze of the microchip, the minimal curve of aerodynamic design."[20] Indeed, machines have been replaced by systems, and the microelectronic circuitry of computers bears little resemblance to the thrusting pistons and grinding gears that characterize industrial machinery. D'Alessandro asks, "What is sensual, erotic, or exciting about electronic tech?" She answers by suggesting that cybernetics makes possible the thrill of control over information and, for the corporate executives who own the technology, control over the consumer classes.

A brilliant example of new technology providing sexually charged power is found in William Gibson's novel *Virtual Light*, which draws a connection between the use of electronic technology for erotic purposes and its use for economic purposes. In the novel a courier is traveling with two "virtual light" glasses; one pair of glasses, his own, provides a virtual sexual experience, and the other pair, which he is delivering, reveals a secret plan to rebuild San Francisco. The erotic charge offered by the first pair is implicitly linked to the thrill of seeing in the second pair how one could make a huge profit in real estate in the new city. As one character tells another who does not "get it," "You never will. But the people who know where to buy, the people who've seen where the footprints of the towers fall, they *will*, Rydell. They'll get it *all*."[21]

The revelation that the virtual light glasses revealing the new city design have been stolen leads to an all-out hunt for the thief and a trail of violence and murder. The courier is the first one killed, not only because he lost the glasses but also because he transgressed by putting them on and looking at the plans for the new cityscape. Ironically, it is the real estate glasses, not the erotic ones, that are taboo. Economic power has been invested with the forbidden thrill traditionally associated with sex.

The previously discussed anonymity offered by electronic technology promises added erotic excitement. Computer sex and other virtual encounters allow users to express their sexual fantasies without revealing their names, faces, or any other characterizing information. One's online persona may bear little or no resemblance to one's physical self, so it becomes possible to express fantasies involving all kinds of personal transformations. Gender becomes fluid: men can interact as women or vice versa, and desire can be unleashed into the electronic realm from the comfortable safety of an anonymous identity.

Popular culture's cyborg imagery also suggests that electronic technology is erotic because it makes possible escape from both the confines of the body and the boundaries that have separated organic from inorganic matter. Robots represent the acclaim and fear evoked by industrial-age machines' ability to function independently of humans, but cyborgs incorporate rather than exclude humans, and in so doing they erase the distinctions that previously were assumed to distinguish humanity from technology. Transgressed boundaries, in fact, define the cyborg. When humans interface with computer technology in popular culture, the process involves transforming the self into something entirely new, combining technological with human identity. Although human subjectivity is not lost in the process, it is significantly altered. As Scott Bukatman notes, "What is at stake in science fiction is no longer the fusion of beings and the immortality of the soul, but the fusion of being and electronic technology in a new, hard-wired subjectivity."[22]

Rather than represent human fusion with electronic devices as terrifying, popular culture frequently represents it as a pleasurable experience. The pleasure of the interface, in Lacanian terms, results from the computer's offer to lead us into a microelectronic Imaginary where our bodies are obliterated and our consciousnesses are integrated into the matrix. The word *matrix*, in fact, originates in the Latin *mater* (meaning mother and womb), and the first of its several definitions in *Webster's Collegiate Dictionary*, 10th ed., is "something within or from which something else originates, develops, or takes form." Computers in pop culture extend to us the thrill of metaphoric escape into the comforting security of our mother's womb, which as Freud explained, represents our earliest home (*heim*). According to Freud, when we have an uncanny (*unheimlich*) response to something, we are feeling the simultaneous attraction and dread evoked by the womb, where we experienced our earliest living moment at the same time that our insentience resembled death.[23] Freud contended that we are constituted by a death wish as well as by the pleasure principle, and pop culture's cyborg imagery effectively fuses the two desires.

The conflicting desires for self-affirmation and self-annihilation figure centrally in the plot of the Borg episodes from the television series *Star Trek: The Next Generation*. The Borg are an alien species that penetrates its members' bodies with technology and replaces their individual identities with a single group consciousness. In the two-part episode "The Best of Both Worlds," the Borg capture Captain Picard, turning him into one of their own by taking over his mind and fusing his body with technological components. They attempt to use his knowledge to defeat the starship *Enterprise* and absorb all of humanity. While Picard is on the Borg ship, the crew members of the *Enterprise* ponder his status; has his transformation into a Borg destroyed his identity, or is he still himself, albeit in an altered state? The admiral of the starship fleet declares Picard dead and promotes Commander Riker to captain of the *Enterprise*. When the *Enterprise's* crew members recapture Picard and return him to his ship, they find that Picard has been transformed into a Borg named Locutus, his face and body pierced by apparatus. He tells them that their resistance is futile. In a last-minute attempt to rescue humankind from the Borg, Lieutenant Commander Data, an android, interfaces by "neural link" with Picard/Locutus and, by extension, the rest of the Borg. Data plants a command in the Borgs' electronic consciousness that puts them to "sleep," a mode they adopt for regeneration. In response the Borg ship self-destructs, and Picard is returned to himself.

The episode's subplot involves a conflict between two ways of life: ambitious individualism versus self-sacrificial loyalty to a group. Commander Riker's authority is challenged by a newcomer, Commander Shelby, an ambitious woman who disregards his commands and announces her desire to obtain his position as second in command of the *Enterprise*. She accuses Riker of playing it safe and getting in her way. Riker has been offered the command of his own ship, but throughout the two-part episode he is torn between his ambition and his loyalty to the *Enterprise*. When he is forced to take the helm of the *Enterprise* following Picard's abduction by the Borg, he initially resists taking charge and suffers from guilt over usurping Picard's authority. He eventually pulls himself together to inspire his crew and devise a strategy to defeat the Borg and save humanity. At the end, however, after Picard has resumed his command, Riker has still not announced whether he will leave the *Enterprise* to command his own ship or remain on board as Picard's subordinate.

Riker's indecision reveals the appeal of interdependence; he knows that everyone, including Picard, expects him to take the new assignment, but he is reluctant to abandon his comfortable niche in the *Enterprise* hierarchy. He understands that commanding a ship carries risks, a fact that becomes clear when the Borg annihilate the ship Riker had been offered. A safe alternative would be to remain under Picard's benevolent leadership.

The episode's two plots stage similar conflicts between autonomy and dependence. Riker's dilemma is mirrored by the relationship of Picard, and all of humanity, to the Borg. There is an undeniable attraction to the smooth workings of an interconnected group, whether it is the crew of the *Enterprise* or the Borg. The communal life is seductive, even though—or perhaps because—it involves a loss of individualism. Picard's transformation into a Borg absolves him of all responsibility; he becomes a Borg emissary without an independent will of his own. There is security in his dependent status, just as there is comfort in the womblike maze of the Borg ship, where the Borg plug into the maternal ship's body for sustenance. When Picard/Locutus unexpectedly makes contact with Data and utters the words "Sleep Data," it becomes apparent that a small part of Picard's consciousness remains submerged within Locutus and that Picard's loyalty is with the *Enterprise*. Ultimately he chooses authority based on a patriarchal model on board the *Enterprise* over submission to the Borg's matriarchal hive society, but the episode nonetheless has presented the seductive appeal of the technological interface.

Subsequent episodes increase the implication that Picard's abduction by the Borg was a type of seduction. Picard resists talking about his experience with the Borg, as if he were ashamed of a sexual transgression. His encounter with the Borg was clearly more than a run-of-the-mill meeting with space aliens; it unsettled Picard deeply and left a lingering sense of attraction combined with repulsion.

Popular culture often represents a collapse of the boundary between human and technological as a sexual act. By associating a deathlike loss of identity with sexuality, pop culture's cyborg imagery upholds a long-standing tradition of using loss of self as a metaphor for orgasm. It is well known that love and death are inextricably linked in the Western cultural tradition, as Denis de Rougemont shows in his book *Love in the Western World*. The equation of death with love has been accompanied in literature by the idea of bodiless sexuality; two united souls represent the purest form of romance. De Rougemont considers the legend of Tristan and Iseult to be Western culture's paradigmatic romantic myth from the twelfth century into the twentieth century. The love between Tristan and Iseult is constantly thwarted by obstacles, and the legend ends in their tragic deaths. De Rougement shows that their passion depends on obstacles; it would be extinguished if it were domesticated by marriage. Furthermore, explains de Rougement, the idea of passionate love immortalized in the legend and embraced by Western culture ever since is a veiled wish for death, the greatest and most irrevocable obstacle. As de Rougement writes,

"From desire to death via *passion*—such has been the road taken by European romanticism; and we are all taking this road to the extent that we
accept—unconsciously of course—a whole set of manners and customs
for which the symbols were devised in courtly mysticism."[24]

The link between death and eroticism is also the subject of Rudolph
Binion's book *Love beyond Death*. Binion argues that prior to the nineteenth century there was an interest in "spiritual love beyond death," but
that nineteenth-century high culture displayed widespread fascination with
"carnal love beyond death." Numerous examples from nineteenth-
century literature and the visual arts intertwine sex and death. "Death,"
writes Binion, "was a piquant aphrodisiac." Necrophilic desire is sometimes hidden below the surface, sometimes overt and unmistakable. According to Binion, after 1914 the theme of erotic death gradually left high
culture and was enthusiastically taken up by popular culture, where it
continues to flourish in films, fiction, music, and comic books.[25]

Pop-culture cyborg imagery that associates the human-computer interface with sexual pleasure is thus part of the long tradition of erotic death
in the arts. Instead of depicting us as losing our consciousness and experiencing bodily pleasures, however, cyborg imagery in pop culture often
invites us to experience sexuality by losing our bodies and becoming pure
consciousness. One of many examples is provided by the comic book
Cyberpunk.[26] Topo, the comic book's protagonist, mentally enters the "Playing Field," a consensual hallucination where all the world's data exists in
three-dimensional abstraction (called "cyberspace" in the cyberpunk novels of William Gibson), saying, "it's the most beautiful thing in the human universe. If I could leave my meat behind and just live here. If I
could just be pure consciousness I could be happy." While in the Playing
Field he meets Neon Rose, a plant-woman with a rose for a head and two
thorny tendrils for arms (and like Topo, present only through the imagination). Even her name inscribes the collapse of boundaries between
organic plant life and a technological construct. Topo engages her in a
contest of wills, represented as their bodies entwined around each other,
while he narrates, "In here, you're what you will. Time and space at our
command. No limits, except how good your software is. No restraints."

Fig. 5. Topo enters the computer matrix in the comic
book *Cyberpunk,* book 1, volume 1, number 1,
September 1989 (story copyright © 1995 Scott Rockwell /
art copyright © 1988 Darryl Banks).

Topo's spoken desire—to leave his meat behind and become pure consciousness, which is in fact what he has done—is contradicted by the imagery: his body—his meat—wrapped around another body.

The word *meat* is widely used to refer to the human body in cyberpunk texts. Meat typically carries a negative connotation in cyberpunk, along with its conventional association with the penis. It is an insult to be called meat in these texts, and to be meat is to be vulnerable. Nevertheless, despite its aversion to meat, *Cyberpunk* visually depicts Topo's body after he has abandoned it to float through the Playing Field's ever-changing topography. His body, however, only seems to be inside the Playing Field because of an illusion, and he is capable of transforming his appearance in any way he desires. As he sees Neon Rose approach, he transforms himself into mechanical parts shaped like his own human body, only more formidable. He has lost his flesh and become steel. Only his face remains unchanged, and it is protected by a helmet. Topo's new powerful body, a product of his fantasy, inscribes the conventional signifiers of masculinity: he is angular with broad shoulders and chest, and most importantly, he is hard. It is no accident that he adopts this appearance to greet Neon Rose, who is coded in clichéd feminine fashion as a sinewy plant who throws her tendrils like lassos, trying to wrap them around him. In case the reader is still unsure of Neon Rose's gender, *Cyberpunk* shows her as a woman after Topo defeats her in their mock battle.

This example from *Cyberpunk* illustrates that although pop culture enthusiastically explores boundary breakdowns between humans and computers, gender boundaries are treated less flexibly in the same texts. Cyberbodies, in fact, tend to appear masculine or feminine to an exaggerated degree. We find giant, pumped-up pectoral muscles on the males and enormous breasts on the females, or in the case of Neon Rose, clichéd flower imagery meant to represent female consciousness adrift in the computer matrix.

Even so, sexual identity is not entirely rigid in cyberpunk texts; there are texts that experiment with sexual instability. In the George Alec Effinger trilogy (*When Gravity Fails, A Fire in the Sun,* and *The Exile Kiss*), for example, surgically altered "sexchanges" are not uncommon. The girl-

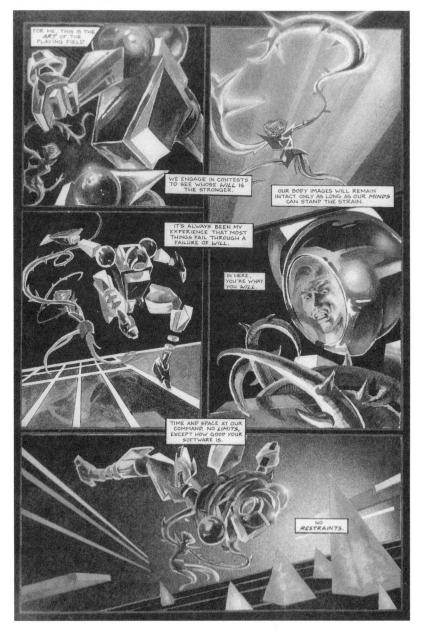

Fig. 6. Topo wrestles with Neon Rose in a battle of wills
in the comic book *Cyberpunk*, book 1, volume 1,
number 1, September 1989 (story copyright © 1995
Scott Rockwell / art copyright © 1988 Darryl Banks).

friend of Marid Audran, the protagonist, is a sexchange named Yasmin, and one of Marid's male acquaintances was once a woman.[27] In Walter Jon Williams's *Hardwired*, too, bodies can be deceptive. In the example mentioned in the last chapter, a wealthy and corrupt old man has had his personality transferred into the body of an innocent-looking young woman.[28]

Despite the fact that people alter their sexual identities in these examples, however, the texts do not radically restructure relations between the sexes. Men and women, whether their sexual identities are natural or surgically created, relate to each other in conventionally patriarchal ways, with men in positions of authority over women. In fact, in the Effinger trilogy, the sexchanges who have chosen to become women typically work as prostitutes in the decadent Budayeen. The male-dominated social system has not changed, even though people have more freedom to situate themselves where they choose within the established order.

Cyborg imagery so far has not widely realized the ungendered ideal Donna Haraway theorizes.[29] Haraway praises the cyborg as a potentially liberatory concept, for it provides a metaphor for gender obsolescence. When gender ceases to be an issue, she explains, women can be released from their inequality under patriarchy and equality becomes possible. Although Haraway does not propose literally replacing gendered bodies with cyborgs, she finds the cyborg a useful concept for illustrating the possibility of an egalitarian social arrangement. Haraway has revised some of the points in her original "Manifesto," especially her sweeping statements about how technology has already become an inseparable part of human life. She says in an interview with Andrew Ross and Constance Penley that her original phrase "we are all cyborgs" is problematic, for it effaces differences between work performed by privileged women in first-world countries and disfranchised women in third-world nations who work in factories producing microelectronic components. In retrospect, she says, she would be "much more careful to point out that those are subject positions for people in certain regions of transnational systems of production that do not easily figure the situations of other people in the system."[30]

Nonetheless, Haraway's "Manifesto" still stands as a unique vision of future technological and social developments.

In addition to speculating about the future, Haraway's essay analyzes feminist science fiction by Joanna Russ, Samuel Delany, John Varley, Octavia Butler, and Vonda McIntyre that provides an alternative to the male fantasies traditionally played out in the genre. Feminist science fiction experiments with unstable categories, unlike the rigidity associated with conventional science-fiction futures that retain or even strengthen the gender stereotypes of the present. Film scholar Janet Bergstrom points out that exaggerated genders dominate in science fiction because "where the basic fact of identity as a human is suspect and subject to transformation into its opposite, the representation of sexual identity carries a potentially heightened significance, because it can be used as the primary marker of difference in a world otherwise beyond our norms."[31]

In heightening gender difference popular culture's cyborg imagery has not caught up with scientist Hans Moravec, who tells us that there will be no genders in the mobile computers that will retain human mental functions on software once the human body has become obsolete, except perhaps "for some theatrical reason. I expect there'll be play, which will be just another kind of simulation, and play may include costume parties."[32] According to Jean-François Lyotard, on the other hand, the most complex and transcendent thought is made possible by the force of desire, and therefore, "thinking machines will have to be nourished not just on radiation but on irremediable gender difference."[33]

Jean Baudrillard takes a similar position when he writes that its inability to feel pleasure makes artificial intelligence incapable of replicating human intelligence.[34] Unlike Lyotard, however, Baudrillard does not insist that gender difference is indispensable. Instead, he sees the collapse of clear boundaries between humans and machines as part of the same postmodern move toward uncertainty that characterizes the collapse of difference between genders. Baudrillard appropriates (some might say misappropriates) a scientific idea to announce that "science has anticipated this panic-like situation of uncertainty by making a principle of it."[35] Indeed, uncertainty is a central characteristic of postmodernism and the essence of the cyborg. Since most cyborgs in pop culture exhibit definite gender difference, however, it is apparent that patriarchy continues to uphold gender difference despite its willingness to relinquish other previously sacrosanct categories.

Even though cyborg imagery in popular culture often exaggerates conventional gender difference, it does not always conform entirely to traditional sexual representations. Whereas most sexual imagery has been designed for a male gaze and has privileged heterosexual encounters, cyborg imagery, taken as a whole, implies a wider range of sexualities. Erotic interfacing is, after all, purely mental and nonphysical; it theoretically allows a free play of imagination. Accordingly, not all cyborg imagery adheres strictly to the standardized male fantasies celebrated in *Playboy*. Neither does it posit the computer as female only in the way that the film *Metropolis* associates technology with female sexuality and represents men as vulnerable to both. Instead, computers in popular culture's cyborg imagery represent sexual release of various kinds for both genders.

In some examples the act of interfacing with a computer matrix is acknowledged to be solitary, but it is nonetheless represented as a sexual act, a masturbatory fantasy expressed in terms of entering something but lacking the presence of another human body or mind. In the comic book *Interface* the interfacing experience of a woman named Linda Williams (interestingly, and perhaps not coincidentally, the name of a film scholar who has written about pornographic films) is coded as masturbation, which becomes linked to the process of thinking.[36] Williams is seen from a high angle lying supine on her bed, saying, "I relax my body. My mind starts to caress the frequencies around me. There. That's better. I'm one with the super-spectrum now. I'm interfaced with the world." In the last panel she is seen doubled, her second self rising nude from the bed with head thrown back and arms outstretched in a sexual pose.

Linda Williams's mental journey through the computer matrix in search of valuable files is drawn to show her nude body diving through oceans of electronic circuitry and a jumble of newspaper headlines. Although female masturbation is a staple of conventional pornography for a male

FIG. 7. Linda Williams sprawls on her bed in order to establish an interface with the "super-spectrum" in the comic book *Interface*, issue 1 (story copyright © 1989 James D. Hudnall / art copyright © 1989 Paul Johnson).

spectator, Williams's interface/masturbation is drawn differently from the norm; her body is ghostly white and in constant motion as she swoops through the matrix surrounded by a watery mist. In two panels her body is merely an indistinct blur. Her body's activity distinguishes her from the conventional passive object of pornography, and her masturbation is not a prelude to heterosexual sex. Later in the evening, after she has returned from the matrix (sighing, "coming down from the interface makes me feel dizzy") and is once again fully clothed, she rejects the sexual advances of a male character. She tells him, "I need some time to myself right now." When he tries to persuade her, she responds, "Not tonight. I know you were expecting me to sleep with you, to make you want to stay. But I don't do that sort of thing. Look, I'm attracted to you. So maybe you'll get lucky sometime. Right now, I've got a lot on my mind. There's so much I have to think about." Williams takes control over her own sexuality, which embodies the cyborgian condition as represented in popular culture by being purely cerebral and simultaneously sexual. When she says that she wants to be alone because there is so much she has to think about, the reader can infer that her private thoughts will be expressed sexually, as they were when she mentally entered the computer matrix.

Imaginary sex—sex without physically touching another human—prevails in cyborg discourses, although bodily sex is not altogether absent. The emphasis on cerebral sexuality suggests that although pain is a meat thing, sex is not. Historical, economic, and cultural conditions have facilitated human isolation and the evolution of cerebral sex. Capitalism has always separated people from one another with its ideology of rugged individualism. Its primary form of sanctioned unity—the nuclear family—traditionally has decreed that one person, usually the woman, relinquish her individuality to support in the private realm the public endeavors of the other person. Public relations under capitalism are characterized by competition and its attendant suspicions. In late capitalism social relations are mediated not only by money but also by the media and its simulations. Rather than communicate, we spectate.

Television viewing literally becomes sacred in William Gibson's *Vir-*

tual Light; a religious cult has formed around a preacher who claims that God manifests himself on television. Cult members stay at home and watch television with great reverence: "What they mostly watch is all these old movies, and they figure if they watch enough of them, long enough, the spirit will sort of enter into them."[37]

Computer technology offers greater opportunities for dialogue — through on-line services and the Internet — than does television, and it can be thought of as a way to reestablish the human contact that was lost during the television decades. It is hardly astonishing that, at a time when paranoia over human contact in response to the AIDS virus is common, human interaction should occur through computerized communication, with the participants far apart and unable to touch each other.

To say that people communicate via their computers is not to say that the act of communication has remained unchanged from the precomputer era. In fact, Jean Baudrillard claims that the term *communication* is imprecise. He writes that in the interface with the computer,

> *the Other, the sexual or cognitive interlocutor, is*
> *never really aimed at — crossing the screen evokes*
> *the crossing of the mirror. The screen itself is*
> *targeted as the point of interface. The machine*
> *(the interactive screen) transforms the process of*
> *communication, the relation from one to the*
> *other, into a process of commutation, i.e., the*
> *process of reversibility from the same to the same.*
> *The secret of the interface is that the Other is*
> *within it virtually the Same — otherness being*
> *surreptitiously confiscated by the machine.*[38]

Although the computer invites us to discard our identities and embrace an imaginary unity, it also, like a mirror, reminds us of our presence by displaying our words back to us. What Baudrillard argues is that this intensely private experience precludes actual interaction with another person and turns all computerized communication into a kind of auto-communication that may contain elements of autoeroticism.

In an example of solitary sexual communion with technology, William Gibson uses the term *jack in* to describe the moment when a "cowboy" sitting at a "deck" enters his command to be transported mentally into cyberspace. (He initially wanted to title his first novel *Jacked In*, but the publisher refused on the grounds that it sounded too much like "Jacked Off.")[39] Gibson's trilogy—*Neuromancer, Count Zero,* and *Mona Lisa Overdrive*—evokes a dystopian future where isolated individuals drift in and out of each other's lives and often escape into fantasy.[40] Not unlike television's mass-produced fantasies of today, Gibson's "simstim" (simulated stimulation) feeds entertaining narratives directly into people's minds. Cyberspace, too, is a place of the mind, but it feels like three-dimensional space to those who enter it: "Cyberspace. A consensual hallucination experienced daily by billions of legitimate operators, in every nation, by children being taught mathematical concepts. . . . A graphic representation of data abstracted from the banks of every computer in the human system. Unthinkable complexity. Lines of light ranged in the nonspace of the mind, clusters and constellations of data. Like city lights, receding . . ."[41]

Jacking into cyberspace metaphorically evokes a heterosexual encounter between a male operator and a female body, for as Nicola Nixon points out, cyberspace can be interpreted as feminine. Lean console cowboys in Gibson's trilogy penetrate cyberspace and encounter obstacles there that threaten their manhood: "The console cowboys may 'jack in,' but they are constantly in danger of hitting ICE (Intrusion Countermeasures Electronics), a sort of metaphoric hymeneal membrane which can kill them if they don't successfully 'eat through it' with extremely sophisticated contraband hacking equipment in order to 'penetrate' the data systems of such organizations as T-A (Tessier-Ashpool)."[42]

Cyberspace is also feminized by the mysterious ghostly figures who inexplicably materialize there. Nixon writes that these otherworldly figures are primarily female, listing as examples 3Jane, Slide, Angie Mitchell, and Mamman Brigitte, a voodoo feminine artificial intelligence. Additionally, certain females have direct mental access to cyberspace, bypassing the equipment required by the male cowboys. Nixon writes, "Constituting both what is fascinating and generative about the matrix itself and the means of accessing its secrets, the feminine is effectively the 'soft' ware, the fantasy (and world) that exists beyond the 'hard' ware of the actual technological achievements in the silicon chip."[43]

Nixon goes on to argue that Gibson's trilogy constitutes cyberspace as a formerly masculine realm that became feminine, a transformation that occurs in *Neuromancer* and is known in the later novels as "When It Changed." Nonetheless, writes Nixon, Gibson's console cowboys enter cyberspace with the energetic determination to reconquer it. Cyberspace is thus a contested realm where a battle for dominance is fought between genders possessing conventional attributes: speedy young male hotshots oppose amorphous women with mysterious powers.

What is ironic about the brash young men who thrust themselves into the metaphorically feminine matrix is that, sexual imagery notwithstanding, they are completely passive and immobile. This is a gendered fantasy of conquest for the electronic age, when television and computers have increasingly confined people to their homes or their work desks; human mobility is in decline.

Cyberpunk fiction explicitly transforms the passivity induced by electronic technology into forceful energy. Case, in *Neuromancer,* is an "interface cowboy" who, when jacked into his deck, runs "in earth's computer matrix." Gibson turns the bodily inactivity that results from the purely cerebral operation of a deck into a sensation of intoxicating movement. Case has "operated on an almost permanent adrenaline high, a byproduct of youth and proficiency, jacked into a custom cyberspace deck that projected his disembodied consciousness into the consensual hallucination that was the matrix. A thief, he'd worked for other, wealthier thieves, employers who provided the exotic software required to penetrate the bright walls of corporate systems, opening windows into rich fields of data."[44] His exuberant roaming over the cyberspace range comes to an end when he steals from his employers, who respond by damaging his nervous system with a "wartime Russian mycotoxin." Gibson writes that for Case, "who'd lived the bodiless exultation of cyberspace, it was the Fall. In the bars he'd frequented as a cowboy hotshot, the elite stance involved a certain relaxed contempt for the flesh. The body was meat. Case fell into the prison of his own flesh."[45]

It is easy to forget, while reading the passages devoted to Case's exhilarating flights into cyberspace after he has recovered from the damage to his nerves, that his body remains absolutely immobile:

Headlong motion through walls of emerald
green, milky jade, the sensation of speed beyond
anything he'd known before in cyberspace. . . .
The Tessier-Ashpool ice shattered, peeling away
from the Chinese program's thrust, a worrying
impression of solid fluidity, as though the
shards of a broken mirror bent and elongated as
they fell —
*   "Christ," Case said, awestruck, as Kuang*
twisted and banked above the horizonless fields
of the Tessier-Ashpool cores, an endless neon
cityscape, complexity that cut the eye, jewel
bright, sharp as razors.[46]

A similar phenomenon occurs in Walter Jon Williams's novel *Hardwired*, where the rush of a moving vehicle substitutes for bodily activity. Users of electronic technology roam freely in the novel when they interface with vehicles—panzers on the ground or supersonic deltas in the air—and ride at incredible speeds without having to use their hands to operate the controls. Cowboy is a "panzerboy" and "delta flyer" who plugs his vehicles' jacks directly into five sockets implanted in his head. Williams writes, "he's living in the interface again, the eye-face, his expanded mind racing like electrons through the circuits, into the metal and crystal heart of the machine."[47] Cowboy virtually becomes the machine; his mind experiences its every shudder as well as its blazing speed. While his body remains immobile, "his muscles will be exercised by electrode to keep the blood flowing. In the old days, before this technique had been developed and the jocks were riding their headsets out of Earth's well and into the long diamond night, sometimes their legs and arms got gangrene." Now, however, "his body will be put to sleep while he makes his run through the Alley. He is going to have more important things to do than look after it."[48]

The novels distract from the actual bodily inertia of Case and Cowboy by emphasizing their flights of cerebral speed. In cyberpunk fiction, as cultural critic Andrew Ross points out, technologically enhanced male bodies tend to be "spare, lean, and temporary," subject to frequent alterations provided by "boosterware, biochip wetware, cyberoptics, bioplastic circuitry, designer drugs, nerve amplifiers, prosthetic limbs and organs, memoryware, neural interface plugs and the like." These mutable cyborg bodies, argues Ross, are a significant departure from the "unadorned body fortress of the Rambo/Schwarzenegger physique" and signal a weakening of the myth of masculine omnipotence.[49]

Even though cyberpunk fiction's male protagonists are not the muscle-bound superheroes I discuss in chapter 4, they still give us an idealized version of the electronic interface, one based on speed rather than muscle. Moreover, adding to their appeal, their characterizations are borrowed from the generic conventions of the western, hard-boiled detective, and film noir traditions. These traditions add a sense of hardness and toughness to divert attention from what is actually the console cowboy's non-physical way of life. Console cowboys display the laconic style and isolation of the western hero. Cowboy, moreover, embodies the western hero's tragic paradox: he achieves legendary status, but at the expense of his value to the community. At the end his services are no longer needed: "He hadn't expected this, to be informed of his obsolescence in a recovery bed on some sweaty Nevada dude ranch. That all he had done, the legend he had built, was only to put him out of business."[50]

Cyberpunk's dark, bleak surroundings and its convoluted plot twists that often involve treachery and betrayal are derived from the cynical world of film noir. Case, Cowboy, and Marid Audran in the Effinger trilogy are involved, like the hard-boiled noir detective, in breaking a case, using electronic technology to gather data. Many of the novels revolve around sleazy urban dives and terse, hard-boiled dialogue. Case and Marid are streetwise and frequent low-life bars. Cowboy is more explicitly associated with the wide-open plains of the West, but the novel borrows a hard-boiled convention when it tells us that he "is twenty-five, getting a little old for this job, approaching the time when even hardwired neural reflexes begin to slacken."[51] It is Sarah, an urban "dirtgirl" who becomes allied with Cowboy, who habituates the seedy bars associated with the hard-boiled genre.

Popular culture's cyborg imagery thus engages in wish fulfillment in the realm of fantasy; it allows inactive humans to feel vigorous and mobile. The GURPS *Cyberpunk High-Tech Low-Life Roleplaying Sourcebook*, a densely elaborate manual for a cyberpunk game, explains the appeal of cerebral flight through cyberspace: "This is *cyberspace*, the world of the *serious* netrunners—data pirates who wire themselves into the net and risk having their brains fried like an egg, all to bring down that near-mythical "big score" that will set them up for life. Of course, some aren't in it for the money—they're addicted to the rush; the tingle of adrenaline flooding their nervous system. In short, they're along for the ride."[52] When console cowboys race through space at lightning speeds, they provide us with heightened feelings of energy. When the space they traverse is the mental realm of cyberspace, they give us the sensation of increased alertness— mental energy—that releases us from feeling mentally sluggish. And the muscular cyborg imagery in films and comic books that I analyze in chapter 4 provides us with the feeling of power and the fantasy of invincibility.

The ultimate fantasy underlying cyborg discourses in both science and pop culture is the wish for immortality. In cyberpunk fiction not even death is certain, thus taking the postmodern principle of uncertainty to its radical extreme. William Gibson and Rudy Rucker have made immortality a central theme in their books, raising questions about whether non-physical existence constitutes life and, especially in Gibson's novels, examining how capitalism might allow only the extremely wealthy class to attain immortality by using technology inaccessible to the lower classes. But cyberpunk fiction is not without recognition of the paradoxes and dangers of immortality. In both Gibson's and Rucker's novels, characters who attempt to become immortal are usually surrounded by a tragic aura of loneliness and decay.

Even Topo, in the comic book *Cyberpunk*, initially rejects the idea of leaving his meat behind and remaining permanently in the Playing Field when he is given the opportunity. What he rejects is immortality. The comic book reveals that the loss of his human body would be tantamount to death, for the invitation to join those who have permanently abandoned their bodies comes from a death mask called The Head that addresses him from atop a pedestal. During their conversation disembodied skulls swoop by around them, reinforcing the death imagery.

When Topo unintentionally loses his human body and becomes a cyberghost trapped in the Playing Field, the line between life and death becomes more ambiguous.[53] There is much speculation among his friends outside the computer matrix about whether Topo is dead or alive. Topo himself, warming up to his new identity, says, "after all, I'm only a data construct myself, now. Nothing equivocal about it. We live. We are forms of life, based on electrical impulses. Instead of carbon or other physical matter. We are the next stop."

Cyborg imagery revolves around the opposition between the creation and destruction of life, expressing ambivalence about the future of human existence. Fusion with electronic technology represents a paradoxical desire to preserve human life by destroying it. Neither alive nor dead, the cyborg in pop culture is constituted by paradoxes; its contradictions are its essence, and its vision of a discordant future is in fact a projection of our conflictual present. What is really being debated in the discourses surrounding a cyborg future are contemporary disputes concerning gender and sexuality, with the future providing a blank screen on which people

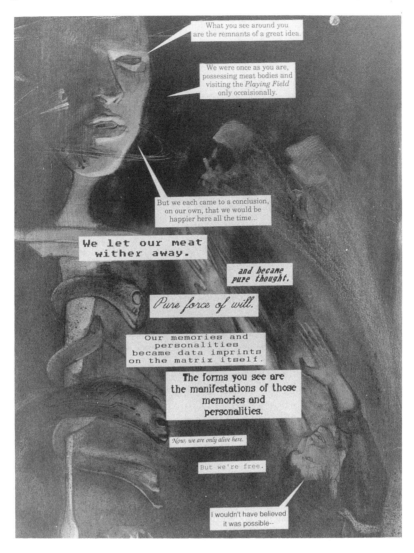

Fig. 8. The Head invites Topo to remain in the computer matrix permanently in the comic book *Cyberpunk*, book 2, volume 1, number 1 (story copyright © 1990 Scott Rockwell / art copyright © 1990 Doug Talalla).

can project their fascination and fears. Whereas some texts cling to traditional gender roles and circumscribed sexual relations, others experiment with alternatives. It is perhaps ironic that a debate over gender and sexuality finds expression in the context of the cyborg, an entity that makes sexuality, gender, and humankind itself anachronistic. Foucault's statement that "man is an invention of recent date. And one perhaps nearing its end" prefigures the consequences of a cyborg future.[54] Nevertheless, as Foucault also argues, it is precisely during a time of discursive crisis, when categories previously taken for granted become subject to dispute, that new concepts emerge. Late-twentieth-century debates over sexuality and gender roles have thus contributed to producing the concept of the cyborg. Depending on one's stake in the outcome, one can look to the cyborg to provide either liberation or annihilation.

CHAPTER 3

Virtual Sex

Lust
motivates
technology.

Michael Saenz[1]

T HE EPIGRAPH BY MIKE SAENZ, a designer of erotic computer software such as "Virtual Valerie," is born out by the proliferation of references to erotic possibilities in the discourses surrounding virtual reality. VR is by no means the first technological innovation to be aligned with sexual impulses; early filmmaking was motivated in part by a desire to gaze surreptitiously at women's bodies, a phenomenon that Linda Williams has described in her essay "Film Body" and in her book *Hard Core.*[2] The voyeuristic urge that accompanied the dawn of cinema proceeded to exert a strong influence on its subsequent development, contributing to cinematic techniques that have since been conventionalized to form the basis of mainstream film language. Recognizing the Victorian origins of film is thus essential for understanding how the cinema has always been implicated in a shifting nexus of titillation and taboo.

Now, a century after the introduction of moving pictures, we are witnessing a new technology, virtual reality, take shape. Development is still in an early stage, so that what people envision for VR far surpasses anything that is currently possible. The visionary discourses surrounding VR are consequently more interesting than the technology itself. Just as early filmmaking was influenced by Victorian preoccupations, in particular by the psychology of repression, the discourses describing virtual reality reveal the concerns of the postmodern late twentieth century. As does all the computer rhetoric analyzed in this book, VR discourses reveal an intense crisis in modes of subjectivity, a crisis that questions the continued existence of human beings at the same time that it predicts a future of heightened erotic fulfillment. The idea of virtual reality has been invested with a collective dream of disembodied sexuality.

Virtual reality is a concept dating back to the late 1960s that has become fashionable in the 1990s, receiving widespread media coverage while several companies develop its capabilities and design marketing strategies. Virtual reality involves a computer-generated space that people wearing goggles fitted with small video monitors perceive as three dimensional. Gloves connected to the computer allow users to interact with the space and feel as though they are performing physical activities such as walking, driving, flying, or picking up objects. The most sustained use of virtual reality has been by the Defense Department in battle simulation and flight training. It would be inappropriate to call virtual reality an escape from reality, since what it does is provide an alternative reality where "being" somewhere does not require physical presence and "doing" something does not result in any changes outside the virtual system. Virtual reality undermines certainty over the term *reality*, ultimately abandoning it altogether, along with all the other certainties that have been discarded in postmodern times. John Perry Barlow, who writes about the cyberworld and is a cofounder of the Electronic Frontier Foundation, which is dedicated to protecting computer hackers' privacy rights and freedom of speech, calls virtual reality "a Disneyland for epistemologists" and declares that it will "further expose the conceit that 'reality' is a fact . . . delivering another major hit to the old fraud of objectivity."[3]

It is widely recognized that VR is often associated with sex. An article in the *Boston Globe*, for example, bemoans the growing interest in cybersex and predicts that it will replace old-fashioned physical sex in the near future.[4] In an article in the book *Cyberspace* Allucquere Rosanne Stone acknowledges that "erotic possibilities for the virtual body are a significant part of the discussions of some of the groups designing cyberspace systems."[5] John Perry Barlow writes, "there is the . . . sexual thing. I have been through eight or ten Q & A sessions on virtual reality and I don't remember one where sex didn't come up."[6] Mike Saenz comments, "when I explain virtual reality to the uninitiated, they just don't get it. But they warm immediately to the idea of virtual sex."[7]

Just how warm people have gotten to the idea is revealed by Howard Rheingold, author of the book *Virtual Reality*, whose fanciful article on what he called teledildonics became an international sensation nearly overnight. His article, which he originally posted on a computer network, deals with what it might feel like to have a virtual sexual experience wearing a bodysuit lined with tiny vibrators connected to visual displays and auditory hookups. In his scenario any number of people separated by thousands of miles could watch computerized visual representations of each others' bodies in sexual embraces while they communicate via modem, all the while feeling tactile stimulation on their bodies that corresponds precisely to their words and images. Rheingold predicted that teledildonics would revolutionize sexual encounters, as well as our definitions of self:

*Clearly we are on the verge of a whole new
semiotics of mating. Privacy and identity and
intimacy will become tightly coupled into*

something we don't have a name for yet. . . .
What happens to the self? Where does identity
lie? And with our information-machines so
deeply intertwingled [sic] *with our bodily*
sensations, as Ted Nelson might say, will our
communication devices be regarded as 'its' . . .
or will they be part of 'us?'"[8]

Looking back at the aftermath of his article's appearance, Rheingold calls it a "thought experiment that got out of control."[9] He received electronic mail in response to the article just hours after posting it and later got telephone calls from people around the world who thought teledildonics existed and wanted to learn more about it. In Germany, where he was to address a computer convention, he was told that he was a "hot commodity" there because people believed that he was "experimenting with ways to have sex with computers." Rheingold writes, "No wonder the vice presidents who introduced themselves to me were smiling the way they were when they told me they were looking forward to my talk."[10]

Films, too, have disseminated the idea that sex is an integral part of virtual reality systems. The film *Brainstorm* (Trumbull 1983) includes a sequence where a reserved and mild-mannered computer technician has his mind irrevocably altered by a virtual sexual experience with an attractive young blond woman. He appears at first to have been rendered senseless from the shock of the experience, but he recovers to emerge transformed into a gregarious man of leisure. The film *Lawnmower Man* (Leonard 1992) also has an extended sequence involving virtual sex between a young woman and Jobe Smith, a young man whose intelligence has been boosted in VR experiments from far below average to superhuman. In this film the experience traumatizes the young woman, who is left in a permanent state of shock.

In both films virtual sex is more powerful, more all-encompassing, than bodily sex, even though virtual sex is purely cerebral and nonphysical. There is clearly a powerful attraction in contemporary culture to the idea

FIG. 9. Virtual sex in the film *Lawnmower Man.*

of bodiless sexuality. To some extent the phenomenon can be interpreted as a response to the actual vulnerability of the human body in the late twentieth century. As Mark Dery writes, "Man-machine miscegenation— robo-copulation, by any other name—may seem a seductive alternative to the vile body, locus of a postmodern power struggle involving AIDS, abortion rights, fetal tissue, genetic engineering, and nanotechnology."[11] Indeed, the human body faces the possibility of devastation on a massive scale: AIDS, environmental disasters, and nuclear war threaten not only to kill individuals but also to annihilate all human beings. In the face of possible obsolescence, it stands to reason that humans should seek solace in projecting themselves into the future reconstituted as pure intellect, without the burden of imperfect, fragile, and mortal bodies. Nonetheless, although the fantasy abandons the body, it refuses to abandon bodily plea-sures. Instead, paradoxically, it heightens sexuality, so that the bodiless future promises to provide extraordinarily intense sexual gratification. It is a fantasy of heightened fulfillment without the risks.

The debates surrounding virtual reality, however, reveal that there is more at stake than the survival of the species. What is really being debated is the form in which the species will survive, specifically, the definition of gender. Discussions of virtual reality are providing a forum for conflicting views on gender roles, ranging from attempts to rigidify conventional definitions of male and female to the desire to dispense entirely with notions of sexual difference. At the center of the conflict is the postmodern subject, for whom identity is no longer easily determined by traditional patriarchal categories and who either yearns for a return to a system of male superiority or celebrates the release from oppressive and archaic gender constraints.

An article by Michael Heim, author of the book *Electric Language* and consultant to the computer industry, exemplifies the desire for a rule-bound, regulated virtual reality system, one that implicitly evokes a patriarchal order.[12] The article, titled "The Erotic Ontology of Cyberspace," begins by asserting that cyberspace (a synonym for virtual reality) is a "metaphysical laboratory, a tool for examining our very sense of reality" (59). The reality constructed by our electronic culture, argues Heim, combines the Platonic sense of eros with the metaphysics of Leibniz. Plato's theory of the erotic drive explains why computers are invested with an erotic allure in our culture. Eros, according to Plato, operates on a continuum that leads from physical attraction all the way to purely cerebral pursuits, so that the desire for abstract knowledge is an extension of the desire for sexual gratification. Both desires are motivated by a drive to extend our existence beyond the life of our physical bodies by giving birth, either to children or to ideas, both of which can carry on after we have died. Computers, according to Heim, have provided the hardware to push to its extreme the Platonic concept of the disembodied erotic drive, making it possible for humans to abandon their "meat" bodies and exist in a higher realm of abstract ideas.

The nature of existence in the computer matrix, according to Heim, derives from Leibniz's conception of a symbolic logic consisting of discrete bits of information represented by abstract signs. Once released from the ambiguity of regular human language, information could, according to Leibniz, be manipulated quickly and efficiently. Writing in the seventeenth century, Leibniz thus provided the basis for modern computation and electronic circuitry. Leibniz also believed that human knowledge should transcend temporal limitations and emulate a godlike perspective from which it could perceive and understand everything simultaneously. Indeed, according to Heim, our contemporary electronic culture attempts to encode everything, reducing all complexities into instantly accessible and unambiguous pieces of information.

Heim argues that by aligning a Platonic erotic drive with a Leibnizian model of godlike omniscience, virtual reality contains a self-defeating paradox. He writes:

Remove the hidden recesses, the lure of the
unknown, and you also destroy the erotic urge to
uncover and reach further, you destroy the source
of yearning. Set up a synthetic reality, place
yourself in a computer-simulated environment,
and you undermine the human craving to
penetrate what radically eludes you, what is novel
and unpredictable. The computer God's-eye view
robs you of your freedom to be fully human.
Knowing that the computer God already knows
every nook and cranny deprives you of your
freedom to search and discover. (78)

To clarify his point Heim analyzes a passage from William Gibson's *Neuromancer* and writes, "The erotic lover reels under the burden of omniscience. . . . Can the beloved remain the beloved when she is fully known, when she is fully exposed to the analysis and synthesis of binary construction?" (79).

Heim worries that the virtual world might abandon rules designed to stabilize erotic desire into fixed patterns. For Heim, with the loss of physical presence in virtual space comes a loss of responsibility and morality.

Whereas "face-to-face communication, the fleshly bond between people, supports a long-term warmth and loyalty" (76), he fears that we will lose a sense of obligation when we are transformed into the virtual puppets we fashion to represent ourselves in virtual reality. The result, he writes, may be "unprecedented barbarism" (77). He maintains a belief in an authentic, unmediated body and implicitly rejects the notion that self-presentation should be free to transcend the limitations of biologically determined categories.

For Heim, mystery is an essential attribute of a fundamentally unknowable other, not something that might arise from the playful theatricality of equally constituted subjects. His version of eroticism imagines only a one-way flow of desire from subject to object, without any return of desire that would establish a reciprocal pattern between two subjects. His world, like patriarchy, would control the object of desire by ensuring its perpetual otherness. A virtual world that removes the shroud of mystery from the object of desire and reveals another subject holds no interest for Heim, for he says that "the idea of the simultaneous all-at-once-ness of computerized information access undermines any world that is worth knowing. The fleshly world is worth knowing for its distances and for its hidden horizons" (80).

Heim's description of the barbaric landscape, the "man-made information jungle" (77), resembles what Fredric Jameson has identified as the decentered confusion of postmodern architecture.[13] Regarding this bewildering space, where "a maze of activities and hidden byways snakes around with no apparent center" (77), Heim expresses regret that information circulates freely regardless of its value. What he wants is a central clearing house, along the lines of a traditional publishing company, that would determine what is worthwhile. It would function, like a cathedral in a medieval European city, to create unity around an absolute center. Heim yearns for a system of centralized authority that limits our access to information on the basis of a canonical set of aesthetic standards. His is thus a rigidly controlled patriarchal virtual reality where expression is constrained and desire is carefully regulated.

In contrast, in an article titled "Mind Is a Leaking Rainbow," computer animation artist Nicole Stenger envisions a virtual reality where the gender and sexual constraints of the past are blown away in an exhilarating blast.[14] She writes, "It was obvious that an explosion would take place, a Big Bang of the old order that was based on gravity, history, and territory. A whole civilization would become unbalanced" (51). Stenger uses apocalyptic yet jubilant language to celebrate the new world, which "will feel like Paradise" (52). Our perception of everything—space, time, life, death, and, most importantly, identity—will be transformed. She suggests that sexual differences will be obliterated, writing, "We will all become angels, and for eternity! Highly unstable, hermaphrodite angels" (52). Like Donna Haraway, whose cyborg is a metaphor for flexible identities, Stenger embraces the idea of blurred boundaries.[15] Unlike Michael Heim, she welcomes the lack of rules and regulations that would impose a sense of order, for she says that "what we call reality was only a temporary consensus anyway" (53).

The most revealing difference in these contrasting visions of virtual reality is in the authors' choices of metaphoric language. Heim's central metaphor is the medieval church spire, a phallic tower that holds sway over the tightly ordered community surrounding it. Stenger's central metaphor is water, the "world of fluids" (54). According to Klaus Theweleit's *Male Fantasies*, a two-volume study of the German Freikorps troops between the world wars, such feminine fluidity evokes overwhelming dread in the protofascist male soldier, who is the extreme pathological product of patriarchy.[16] Indeed, Nicole Stenger sympathizes sarcastically with the "poor souls that may get drowned in the liquid mirror of their minds and perhaps become females" in VR (54). In addition, taking a jab at one of the foremost theorists of postmodernism, she writes, "Mr. Baudrillard, how can you sell your dry nuts on the shore when we have so much fun in the water!" (54).

Heim and Stenger are joined by others in trying to imagine how electronic sexuality might unfold. Responses to virtual sex range from condemnation to celebration. Some individuals applaud its promise of free sexual expression and emphasize its educational benefits. Author and computer researcher Brenda Laurel says that

we have a new representational world that allows
people to construct representations of their own
sexuality for each other. And these constructions
are no longer bounded by the narrow vocabulary
of real-world fashion and stereotypes. Teenagers,
for instance, generally have a pretty narrow
palette with which to express their sexuality. And
yet we're starting to see opportunities with
computer networks and to some extent interactive
games, to construct flavors of one's sexual
persona that aren't stereotypes, that escape those
cages. I think that's all for the best. The more we
can do to bring our sexual energies to bear in the
emergence of new media paradigms, the better.[17]

Mike Saenz also predicts that virtual sex will have positive educational applications: "Just as a flight simulator is used to train pilots before they climb into a real place, I think sex simulation could be used to prevent unwanted pregnancies and warn about sexually transmitted diseases."[18] He predicts that "sophisticated sex simulation will be ubiquitous and accepted as legitimate entertainment, education and therapy."[19] The result, he hopes, will be "goodbye to a lot of unnecessary pain for a lot of people who don't know how to actually have a personal and intimate relationship."[20] The editor of *Future Sex* magazine, Lisa Palac, and an editor of *Mondo 2000*, Jude Milhon, are among those who envision healthy virtual sexual possibilities. Milhon asserts that cybersex can protect its users from both the physical and psychological dangers of sex between human beings.[21]

Others are less optimistic. Linda Jacobson, editor of *CyberArts*, warns that virtual sex could increase men's abusive power over women: "Smut on paper or video is much more benign than interactive stroke books. These products show men that they can have control over women. You can force them to do your bidding and they do it willingly. I am absolutely opposed to censorship, but I think men have to be made aware that this kind of thing can make women feel very uncomfortable."[22] Author and sex educator Susie Bright expresses mixed feelings about virtual sex; her enthusiasm for its invitation to express erotic fantasies is mixed with concern over who will control the technology:

The computer business and the sexual
entertainment industry are both classically
male-dominated arenas. Were female desires and
perspectives going to be alive in a virtual reality
created by computer nerds? I have my own very
feminine adolescent fantasies to attend to and I
don't imagine that they will be addressed by the
mainstream of this business. Aside from equal
opportunity self-indulgence, I wondered what
kind of virtual software we could look forward to
if it was going to be created by techies with no
social skills or nurturing vision whatsoever.[23]

With an even more pointed critique of the escapism involved in virtual reality, Vivian Sobchack writes that

the emergence of a celebratory (and generally
economically privileged) subculture vacationing
in virtual spaces and practicing a "virtual
politics" (one that doesn't seem greatly to affect
the daily world except by its absence) seems to
me the mark of a potentially dangerous and
disturbingly miscalculated attempt to escape the
material space and specific politics (dare I say

the "real" reality?) of the body's mortality and
the planet's fragility. And this at a time when
everybody needs to pay close attention to our
existential and quite concrete investment in
both.[24]

At the same time, Sobchack is not surprised that the desire to escape into virtual worlds has taken hold as strongly as it has: "In an age in which temporal coordinates are oriented toward computation rather than toward human beings, and spatial coordinates have shrunk to the brief occupation of 'here,' in an age in which there is too much perceived risk to living and too much information for both body and mind to contain and survive, need we wonder at the desire to transcend and escape where and who we are."[25]

The lack of concern over social realities in what has been written about virtual reality troubles Scott Bukatman. He refers to the euphoric claims of VR proponents as "cyberdrool," which, he writes, "is almost blind to ideology: . . . There is little understanding of social process or political understanding revealed in these writings, just an obsolete and naïve liberalism that believes that if we all just *thought about it like reasonable human beings*, societal inequities and the drive for power would evaporate."[26]

Power relations between the sexes are at the heart of pop-culture treatments of virtual sex. The film *Lawnmower Man*, for example, is preoccupied with gender roles. It revolves around the premise that when Jobe's intellect skyrockets to remarkable levels, he is also transformed into a hypermasculine hulk. Jobe's intellectual growth combined with his personality transformation under a scientist's guidance recalls the Pygmalion scenario. In Jobe's case his initial mild and submissive personality, along with his long hair and bib overalls, codes him as effeminate. After his mind has undergone intelligence-boosting experiments in virtual reality, however, his body becomes taut and muscular, he wears tight jeans and boots, and he walks with a cowboy's swagger. The film thus rejects the possibility that Jobe might abandon biological definitions of gender and

Fɪɢ. 10. Jobe Smith is simple-minded and childlike
before becoming the subject of virtual reality
experiments in the film *Lawnmower Man*.

Fɪɢ. 11. Virtual reality turns Jobe into a muscular
he-man in the film *Lawnmower Man*.

FIG. 12. Bodily boundary confusion during virtual sex in
the film *Lawnmower Man*.

experiment with fluid gender boundaries once his mind has been de-
tached from his body in virtual reality. Once he has been transformed,
the film prevents any doubt about his masculinity.

In fact, Jobe's masculinity becomes exaggerated; he turns into a violent
aggressor and goes on a brutal killing spree. The film suggests that when
Jobe's intelligence is boosted, his unconscious savagery also erupts. When
the boundary breakdowns of virtual reality combine with those of sexual
intimacy, as Jobe enters VR to have sex with his girlfriend, his unconscious erupts into sadistic rage. While their bodies remain suspended in
mechanisms that resemble gyroscopes, their minds conjure up virtual
puppet bodies and an ever-changing virtual landscape. During their virtual sexual encounter Jobe's puppet becomes a roaring monster from the
id that terrorizes his trembling girlfriend. Jobe's savage puppet represents
the rage of the patriarchal unconscious. He is transformed into the patriarchal extreme of the fascistic soldier who, according to Klaus Theweleit,
kills in order to maintain a fragile sense of his own bodily boundaries.
Theweleit argues that by destroying other bodies, an individual such as

the Freikorps soldier externalizes the disintegration he fears within himself and temporarily convinces himself that he possesses a stable subjectivity. The fascistic soldier fears a loss of control so intensely that he avoids sex and despises women, onto whom he projects sexual temptation and what he perceives as the dangers of bodily fluidity.

Indeed, Jobe's transformation into a savage killer occurs after he has been threatened with a loss of boundaries from both virtual reality and sex. The film thereby expresses an ambivalent attitude toward virtual reality, on the one hand celebrating it as a playground for the imagination and on the other hand putting up defenses against its inducement to play with gender roles. As the magazine *Mondo 2000* points out, in virtual reality, "it's always impossible to tell for sure the sex, age, color or even species (there are cats here) of the person you're accessing."[27] Allucquere Rosanne Stone goes further when she writes that "to become the cyborg, to put on the seductive and dangerous cybernetic space like a garment, is to put on the female."[28] With its invitation to relinquish boundaries and join the masquerade, virtual reality asks everyone to experience the fluidity of feminized subjectivity. Current debates, however, suggest that before virtual reality becomes a masquerade party, it might first be a battlefield where the struggle over gender roles will be fought behind virtual barricades.

CHAPTER 4

Muscular Circuitry

The whole world is men's bloody fantasies.

Abhor, a cyborg[1]

ROBOCOP AND THE TERMINATOR have smashed their way into the public's awareness in a series of highly successful films. Their features have given concrete shape to the idea of human fusion with technology. Both are aggressively violent cyborgs that embody a fantasy of destructive force combined with invincibility. Although this hyperviolent figure is only one of many types of fictional cyborgs in circulation, it has become the dominant way for mainstream commercial films to represent the cyborg condition. While television, science-fiction literature, and comic books have explored diverse and imaginative ways to depict the fusion of

FIG. 13. Max Headroom grins and giggles inside his
television world in the television film "Twenty Minutes
into the Future."

humans and technological artifacts, mainstream films have privileged the
violently masculinist figure. An analysis of invincible armored cyborg films
reveals that the films and the cyborg bodies they put on display stage a conflict between different ways of thinking about sexual identity and gender.

Whereas the software-interfaced cyborg envisioned by scientist Hans
Moravec would make the human body obsolete once human consciousness has been downloaded onto computer software, the mainstream films
represent cyborgs as aggressive, bulging bodies.[2] The cyborg's physical
prowess is heightened, not abandoned, and its strength is physical, not
cerebral. What these cyborgs do best is kill.

Although such films are more consistent than other pop-culture texts
in depicting cyborgs as aggressive killers, not all cyborgs in films are
hypermasculine killing machines. Moreover, these filmic cyborg killing
machines often have other functions. The Terminator, in fact, functions
as a surrogate father in *Terminator 2*. Nevertheless, many mainstream com-

mercial films remain firmly entrenched in a tradition that upholds conventional sex roles and maintains a stable masculine subject position by constructing a gaze assumed to be male. There are occasional exceptions to the classical Hollywood paradigm, especially outside the commercial mainstream, where some films introduce a high degree of instability and androgyny. In her essay "Androids and Androgyny" Janet Bergstrom analyzes how androgyny in the independently made film *Liquid Sky* (Tsukerman 1982) disrupts conventional expectations concerning sexual difference.[3] And yet, explains Bergstrom, the film also acknowledges that androgyny could no longer successfully challenge the status quo after it had been transformed from a subversive punk statement to a high-fashion style during the late 1970s and early 1980s.

Even when recent mainstream popular films have altered the strategies that prevailed during Hollywood's studio era, they still generally have insisted on difference between their male and female characters. Constance Penley argues that even contemporary science-fiction films, in which androgyny occurs with some frequency, establish a strong sense of difference by creating seemingly insurmountable barriers between characters. Humans become involved in difficult liaisons with aliens, androids, cyborgs, or humans from the future. Penley writes, "In these films the question of sexual difference—a question whose answer is no longer 'self-evident'—is displaced onto the more remarkable difference between the human and the other."[4]

In most mainstream films the principle of difference between men and women still dominates, even when they go beyond mere sexual difference. Other media allow for more flexibility. Television, for example, establishes a more fragmented relationship with the spectator, showing less concern with the conventional cinematic techniques of directing the spectator's gaze and achieving narrative closure. Television theorists have pointed out that its shifting sites of identification and open-ended narratives allow for more flexibility than does conventional mainstream cinema. In the British television film "20 Minutes into the Future," the precursor to the television series *Max Headroom*, a television reporter named

Edison Carter is maimed and subsequently re-created electronically. In his new identity as "Max Headroom," he exists only inside television, framed in the classic newscaster's medium close-up head shot. Media theorist Lynne Joyrich posits that Max Headroom dissolves boundaries in a "feminized" fashion:

Bound to the TV mosaic (fully "in the system" as Max claims to be), the television cyborg achieves a kind of grace and overpresence—an egoless absorption of the patterns on the screen. Thus achieving a harmony of being, the paradoxical holism born of boundary confusion, the cyborg seems to embody an image of femininity which has also been described in terms of empathy and closeness, excess and disruption. Replacing the woman as the cultural sign of contiguity, the television cyborg is then figured as feminized, intimately tied to the flow of a new nature (the technological and TV matrix) as it's plugged into the world.[5]

Max Headroom's playful indulgence in his egoless freedom inside television does not make him a feminist figure, but he does provide an alternative to conventional masculine stereotypes and thus contributes to the collapse of rigid sex roles. Likewise, its fragmentation does not make television a feminist medium, but feminist implications can sometimes emerge from its disruption of classic Hollywood-style seamless narratives and stable diegeses, where the fictional world accommodates no alternatives. Max Headroom is a far cry from the invincible armored cyborgs who cling to masculine stereotypes by fighting off threats of dissolution, relying on violence to maintain their bodily boundaries.

Unlike Max Headroom, RoboCop and the Terminator engage in relentless violence with their technologically fortified bodies. To some extent the phenomenon of the rampaging filmic cyborg suggests a residual fear of technology that found similar expression in older films like *Metropolis*. Electronic technology's incredible capabilities certainly can evoke fear and awe, which can be translated in fictional representation into massive bodies that overpower human characters.

Nonetheless, fear of the computer's abilities does not entirely explain why films consistently associate cyborgs with violence. Significantly, muscle-bound cyborgs in films are informed by a tradition of muscular comic-book superheroes, and like these superheroes, their erotic appeal is in the promise of power they embody. Their heightened physicality culminates not in sexual climax but in acts of violence. Violence substitutes for sexual release. Film scholar Steven Neale has written that violence displaces male sexuality in films in response to a cultural taboo against a homoerotic gaze and that homophobia exerts a strong influence on cinematic techniques.[6] For example, close-up shots that caress the male body on screen encourage a homoerotic response from the male spectator. As Neale explains, however, the spectacle of a passive and desirable male body is typically undermined by a narrative that intervenes to make him the object or the perpetrator of violence, thereby justifying the camera's objectification of his body. The heightened physicality of cinematic cyborgs thus culminates not in sexual expression but in brute force.

The association between technology and violence is not unique to the twentieth century. During the social upheavals of the nineteenth-century Industrial Revolution, when people's lives were radically transformed, widespread optimism that machines would bring progress was accompanied by anxiety about technology's potentially destructive powers. The fear evoked by machines was exacerbated by their sheer magnitude; they were often huge and loud, and they thrust, pumped, and turned with an aggressive persistence. Their power was palpable and visible.

Unlike industrial machinery and its forceful energy, electronic technology functions quietly and passively. Nevertheless, as I stated earlier in this book, industrial-age metaphors for representing technology persist in the information age. For example, computers are compared on the basis of their "power," a term that used to refer to physical strength but now can connote a computer's calculating speed or memory. Thus, operations related to nonphysical computer functions are discursively reconstituted to imply physical force. Our postmodern age is marked by discursive anachronisms that date from the exigencies of the industrial and resolutely patriarchal nineteenth century. Violent, forceful cyborg imagery participates in contemporary discourses that cling to nineteenth-century notions about technology, sexual difference, and gender roles in order to resist the transformations brought about by the new postmodern social order.

Mechanization has not always been conceived of as physically forceful. Historian Roger Hahn points out that from the ancient Greek period until the Renaissance, the uninformed public conceived of mechanization as concealed and mysterious.[7] Most people's understanding of machinery was based on seeing the mechanical automata that were often shaped like humans or animals and designed to amaze them by performing independently of human control. The mechanisms that controlled the automata were hidden from view, and artisans kept their designs a secret to enhance the notion that the figures were magical and mysterious.

During the Renaissance, according to Hahn, there was a shift in the concept of mechanization from internal to external and accessible. Mechanical devices were demystified once they were released from the possessive grip of secret societies. Texts that explained how machines worked, complete with precise illustrations, began to proliferate in the sixteenth century, making such devices comprehensible to all. According to Hahn, "The visual representation of machines forever stripped them of secret recesses and hidden forces."[8] At the same time, the new Renaissance philosophies of scientific inquiry replaced the earlier exaltation of the invisible with an emphasis on the externally visible. Scientists beginning with Bacon and Galileo privileged theories that could be verified through experimentation rather than accepted on pure faith. As Hahn writes, "The tone of the new science was to displace the occult by the visible, the mysterious by the palpable."[9]

The concept of externally forceful machinery culminated in the industrial machinery of the nineteenth and early twentieth centuries. In accordance with the machine's new role as a worker, a new figure, the robot, replaced the automaton as the human being's mechanical double. After the term *robot* was introduced in a play titled *R.U.R.* ("Rossum's Universal Robots"), written by Czech playwright Karel Čapek in 1920,[10] robot imagery became a staple of early-twentieth-century science fiction, which usually maintained the Frankenstein theme enacted in *R.U.R.* by depicting robots as dangerous entities determined to overthrow humanity.[11]

More than a simple name change separated robots from automata. Automata belonged to an earlier time when mechanization was a wonderful and entertaining mystery; robots belonged to the age of factories and mills, when machines forcefully announced their powerful presence. Jean Baudrillard argues that "a whole world separates these two artificial beings," that the automaton is "the analogy of man," whereas the robot "is man's equivalent."[12]

We shouldn't make any mistakes on this matter
for reasons of "figurative" resemblance between
robot and automaton. The latter is an
interrogation upon nature, the mystery of the
existence or non-existence of the soul, the
dilemma of appearance and being. It is like God:
what's underneath it all, what's inside, what's in
the back of it? . . . No such thing with the robot.
The robot no longer interrogates appearance; its
only truth is its mechanical efficacy.[13]

With the transition from automata to robots, the significance assigned to artificial beings underwent a change. Robots were no longer treated as charming mechanical novelties; rather, they were evaluated on the basis of what they were capable of doing, either for humans or to humans.

In the late twentieth century machines have been replaced by systems dependent on intricate microelectronic circuitry. Our information age reintroduces a concept of technology as incomprehensible and hidden from view. Computer hardware contains microscopic parts concealed behind the computer screen, and for most people, how the system functions remains shrouded in mystery. Although there are no secret societies that invest computers with magical properties, computer hardware expertise is nevertheless confined to trained specialists, who often are themselves awed by the intricacy and hidden capacities of computers. According to Bruce Sterling:

Computers are fearsome creations, redolent of
mystery and power. Even to software engineers
and hardware designers, computers are, in some
deep and basic sense, hopelessly baffling. This is
why commercial software is sold without any
kind of real warranty, why computers are buggy,
crashy, fluid, nonlinear and radically unreliable.
Machines that perform millions of interactive
operations per second are simply far too complex
for any human brain to fully comprehend.[14]

Despite the concealed and mysterious intricacy of computers, cyborg imagery in the RoboCop and Terminator films relies on an external rather than an internal concept of mechanization. RoboCop and the Terminator, like robots, are distinguished by their large size and physical power, even though technology has become smaller and more passive since the industrial machines that inspired the idea of the robot. These cinematic cyborgs are aggressively corporeal, and as Mary Ann Doane tells us, "when technology intersects with the body in the realm of representation, the question of sexual difference is inevitably involved."[15]

Cyborg films are in fact preoccupied with sexual difference, and one of their sites of contestation is the figure of the cyborg, whose technologically produced form embodies metaphors of human sexuality: steely hard

phallic strength is opposed to feminine fluidity. These particular metaphors, still prevalent today, derive from ways of thinking that became dominant in the late eighteenth century, when the notion of two distinct and
opposite sexes was naturalized and taken for granted. Earlier, as Thomas
Laqueur documents in his book *Making Sex*, people generally thought in
terms of a one-sex model in which women's bodies were considered to be
less fully developed versions of men's bodies, with genitals that were virtually identical to men's, only inverted rather than distended.[16] The one-sex
system was vertical and hierarchical; women were thought of as less perfect than men but not altogether different from them. The different social
roles assigned to men and women were not justified on the basis of clear-
cut biological difference prior to the late eighteenth century but instead
were understood to be based on culturally defined gender categories. In
fact, the body was not considered to be an entirely reliable indicator of a
person's sex. Laqueur cites numerous stories that circulated before the
eighteenth century about women whose bodies were transformed by the
emergence of a penis; once the transformation had been verified by doctors, these women were allowed to change their names and become men.[17]
Only after the social and political upheavals of the eighteenth century did
the two-sex model triumph, and this change occurred not because of new
knowledge about the human body but because of the requirements of the
ascendant bourgeoisie and their newly industrializing societies.

In the two-sex model that still rules late-twentieth-century thinking, a
woman's difference from men, and her supposed inferiority to them, is
explained by reducing her to her body, specifically, her sexual organs,
which are considered to be the opposite of men's. Women's genitals are
described as hidden, internal, and inert, in contrast to what is described
as the forceful and aggressive male penis. Women are thus associated with
the interior spaces of the body, with the hidden, fluid, and fluctuating
internal systems. (In the one-sex model, Laqueur shows, both men's and
women's bodies were understood to be fluid-filled vessels.)[18] Men in the
two-sex model, on the other hand, are associated with dry solidity and
with hard physical strength.

Masculine and feminine stereotypes have long been used as metaphors for technology, and they are likely to persist as long as the two-sex system prevails. Aggressive, muscular cyborg imagery asserts the dominance of a phallic metaphor for technology. Phallic cyborgs constitute a contrast to the other, contradictory metaphor for contemporary electronic technology: the "feminized" computer with its concealed, passive, and internal workings. Feminine metaphors emphasize that microcircuitry is not physically forceful or massive. Miniaturization, concealment, and silence are its underlying principles. Moreover, computer users often experience a psychological union with their terminals that collapses ego boundaries. The intimacy and empathy that can result from fluid ego boundaries are conventionally associated with feminine subjectivity, which, compared to the male ego, is less dependent on Oedipal individuation. It has recently become somewhat more acceptable in Western societies for men to exhibit so-called feminine traits, so that a fluid ego boundary is no longer thought of as an exclusively feminine characteristic. There are, however, patriarchal bastions of resistance to any human behavior that defies traditional gender stereotypes. The hyperviolent muscular cyborg in films is one such symbol of misogynistic resistance to change. He rampages across the screen as if to deny that late-twentieth-century technology no longer fits the forceful phallic model and that there is now a greater acceptance of human sexual diversity.

It is important to note that feminine metaphors for technology are not necessarily feminist. Like masculine metaphors, they can be used to fortify patriarchal notions about gender difference. In fact, they function this way in the film *Eve of Destruction*, which I discuss later in this chapter.

Although the computer is the dominant technological paradigm for our age, it has not entirely displaced industrial machines. As J. David Bolter writes, "the computer leaves intact many older technologies, particularly the technologies of power, and yet it puts them in a new perspective. With the appearance of a truly subtle machine like the computer, the old power machines (steam, gas, or rocket engines) lose something of their prestige."[19] With both electronic and industrial technologies present in our lives, we are seeing a conflict between ways of conceptualizing technology in gendered terms: masculine metaphors oppose feminine metaphors. Andrew Ross exposes masculine metaphors when he analyzes the boy's sensibility that pervades cyberpunk fiction, which typically uses tough-guy jargon and imagery drawn from hard-boiled detective fiction to describe the human interface with technology.[20] Nicola Nixon also identifies a misogynistic base underlying cyberpunk's technology-laden futuristic dreams when she describes how cyberpunk spokesmen implicitly denigrate feminist science fiction of the 1970s by speaking of cyberpunk's reinvigoration of science fiction during the 1980s following a decade of decline.[21]

Counteracting popular culture's frequent emphasis on technological virility, Donna Haraway conceives of the cyborg as a potentially feminized and feminist figure, one that could make gender difference obsolete and liberate women from patriarchal inequality.[22] Once the cyborg has eliminated the boundary between humans and machines, other traditional hierarchical boundaries, such as the one between the sexes, could also dissolve. Haraway is joined by feminist theorists Avital Ronell[23] and Valie Export[24] in urging women to consider how technology might be used to restructure social relations and notions of the self in feminist ways. They encourage women to reject the technophobic strain of feminism that associates women with the so-called natural world and condemns all technologies for being patriarchal tools of oppression. Haraway stresses the importance of developing an alternative to the politics of domination that controls the world's economic, racial, class, and gender systems. Despite its miniaturization, observes Haraway, electronic technology is currently used in insidiously powerful ways to subjugate workers and create increasingly destructive tools of war.[25] It is thus essential for women to appropriate and redefine technology according to feminist principles. Nineteenth-century social and economic relations have already been transformed in our postmodern era, and Haraway's "Manifesto" urges feminists to embrace the cyborg paradigm rather than allow a new masculine style of late-twentieth-century domination to prevail.

Cyborg films exist within our culture's larger discursive conflict over gendered metaphors for technology. The films sometimes betray signs of confusion when they try to depict a new electronic age using imagery from the industrial past. *The Terminator* reveals its mixed metaphors when it represents the threat that technology poses to human beings. As Constance Penley shows, it forges a link between contemporary household gadgets that tend to malfunction and future high tech that launches a full-scale revolt against humans.[26] In the film the precise nature of technology's danger to humans is identified as its intelligence but depicted as physical violence. Kyle Reese, a character in the film, explains that the war against humanity was masterminded by defense network computers that "got smart, a new order of intelligence," and decided to exterminate all humanity. Nevertheless, the threat is made manifest in the film by the figure of the Terminator, who relies on brute force to destroy humans. Even the depiction of the future shows not defense network computers but tanks, aircraft, and terminators that hunt and kill humans in an industrial wasteland of twisted steel.

The Terminator contains one sequence in particular that reveals how it rejects a feminized cyborg in favor of a hypermasculine one. The Terminator, a cyborg who has been created by his computer masters to travel back through time to 1984 to kill a young woman, Sarah Connor, arrives in 1984 folded on the ground in a fetal position, naked and vulnerable, as if newly born. His vulnerability increases when three punk youths laugh and sneer at his nakedness and brandish switchblades. With incredible force he hurls two of them through the air and enters another with his fist to pull out his heart. He penetrates the youth's body in a sexual way, laying claim to phallic mastery. When we next see him, he is wearing their leather and metal-studded clothing, and soon thereafter he obtains an arsenal of guns. No longer vulnerable, he is now fully armored in the trappings of aggressive masculinity.

The Terminator's nude entrance is repeated by the film's other time traveler, Kyle Reese. Vivian Sobchack makes the following point about their nudity: "Both the Terminator and Reese fall from above the frame of

FIG. 14. Stark naked, the Terminator enters a saloon in the film *Terminator 2: Judgment Day.*

a dirty modern city, their nakedness a designation of their male sexual biology and their alien-ated status." Reese and the Terminator enter the film similarly, but, Sobchack writes, they represent contrasting versions of masculinity in crisis, especially in their styles of fatherhood: Reese is the warm, protective, paternal figure, whereas the Terminator is the obsessive destroyer.[27] The film is one of many from the 1980s that stage the crisis of defining fatherhood amid the changes in family structure brought on by feminism.

In the sequel, *Terminator 2: Judgment Day* (Cameron 1991), the Terminator undergoes the same kind of transformation as in the first film. He arrives from the future stark naked in a womblike bubble. When he enters a tough country-and-western saloon, we observe from his point of view how everyone stares in disbelief at his penis. Only after the Terminator brutally attacks the saloon's patrons and clothes his naked body in a biker's gear does he earn their complete fear and respect. He leaves with the paraphernalia that guarantees his phallic authority: a Harley-Davidson

FIG. 15. Armored in leather and astride a Harley, the
Terminator gets respect in the film *Terminator 2:
Judgment Day.*

Fat Boy motorcycle and a big gun. His equipment is external, displacing
his penis with its symbolic equivalents, thus asserting an externally forceful masculine image of a technological human.

RoboCop also begins his existence in an inert manner appropriate to
electronic technology: he is a computer. What we see from his point of
view is his transformation into a masculine hulk. He is passive as he is
worked on by the Security Concepts team that is creating him by fusing
mechanical and electronic components with some remains of murdered
police officer Alex J. Murphy. The first indication that RoboCop will become something other than a computer terminal is when his creators
display a powerful robotic arm before attaching it to him. After he has
been completed, we see that he has the exaggerated physique of a muscle
man made of steel.

Fusion with the technological in *The Terminator* and *RoboCop*
(Verhoeven 1987) is tantamount to stepping into a suit of armor. Both

cyborgs are represented as invincible humans whose fortified bodies protect them from assaults that would destroy an ordinary human. The Terminator withstands gunfire, car and motorcycle crashes, a tank truck running over him, a fire that burns off all his skin, and an explosion that rips
off his legs. Although finally destroyed when crushed in a hydraulic press,
he is replaced by an identical terminator in *Terminator 2*. RoboCop also
strides fearlessly into blazing gunfire and withstands multiple attacks.
When he is disabled, and even destroyed, he knows that he can be reas-
sembled. As he tells his human partner, Anne Lewis, when she is badly
injured at the end of the film, "They'll fix you; they fix everything."

Unlike cyberpunk fiction's lean, vacillating male bodies, the Terminator and RoboCop display rock-solid masculinity. Their technological adorn-
ments serve to heighten, not diminish, their bodies' status as fortresses.
Cyborg imagery in the RoboCop and Terminator films exemplifies the
invincible armored killing machine theorized by Klaus Theweleit in *Male
Fantasies*.[28] The protofascist soldiers Theweleit analyzes not only kill to
externalize the dissolution of self they fear but also despise women, onto
whom they project fluid ego boundaries and the temptation of sexual
union, with its terrifying prospect of blurred boundaries. They take the
two-sex model to an extreme, fortifying themselves with hard leather and
metal body armor to assert their solidity against the threat of fluid women
and to shore up their own fragile egos. Fascist armored-body imagery has
appeared in many guises and has also been used to critique fascist ideology from within its own discourse, as Hal Foster shows in his analysis of
the works of artists Max Ernst and Hans Bellmer.[29]

For the Freikorps soldiers, invincibility was an unrealizable fantasy.
Cyborgs like the Terminator and RoboCop realize the Freikorps fantasy
in the realm of representation, making possible in fiction what can be
only fantasized in fact. The Terminator methodically stalks his victim
and feels no pain; as his adversary Kyle Reese tells Sarah Connor, "it can't
be bargained with, it can't be reasoned with, it doesn't feel pity or remorse
or fear and it absolutely will not stop, ever, until you are dead." RoboCop
is also a brutal killer, even though his acts of violence are legitimized

FIG. 16. From Robo-Computer's point of view, we see
the Security Concepts' team display the robotic arm
that will be attached to RoboCop in the film *RoboCop*.

FIG. 17. RoboCop has been turned into an armored
man of steel in the film *RoboCop*.

because he is a police officer fighting vicious criminals. When he is re-programmed in *RoboCop 2* to apprehend criminals without killing them, he is ridiculously ineffective. The film celebrates his return to killing when he overcomes the restrictive program.

Theweleit argues that the protofascist fantasy of armored invincibility signifies a desire to ward off external threats of ego absorption and, simultaneously, ego dissolution from within. As if to illustrate the phenomenon, the film *Total Recall* (Verhoeven 1990) revolves around a fragmented subject, Doug Quaid, who suddenly learns that he may not be who he thinks he is and that his identity may be nothing more than an illusion created by an electronic implant in his head. (With a microchip in his head, he qualifies as a cyborg.) The lines between dream and reality, fact and fantasy, become blurred for Quaid as he struggles to discover his true identity—to create a coherent internal self—and to repel attackers who threaten him from all sides, with the most brutal attacks launched by the woman he thought was his wife. Quaid's psychological instability has no visual signifier, however; he is undeniably present and solid as a rock as played by Arnold Schwarzenegger, whose hypermasculine physique has become associated with cyborgs in the public imagination. By the end he has violently destroyed his attackers and heroically saved the human inhabitants of Mars from complete annihilation. Even his moment of doubt at the end, when he fears that all his exploits might have been a dream rather than reality, does not dispel the fantasy of omnipotent power that the film presents.

Doug Quaid, RoboCop, and the Terminator perpetuate and even exaggerate the anachronistic industrial-age metaphor of externally forceful masculine machinery, expressing nostalgia for a time when masculine superiority was taken for granted and an insecure man needed only to look at technology to find a metaphor for the power of phallic strength. Electronic technology no longer evokes the metaphor of externally visible musculature; instead, its bodily equivalents are the concealed and fluid internal systems. Moreover, in their interaction with humans, computers offer a radically new relationship, one that no longer fortifies physical prowess. It is the miniaturization and stasis of electronic technology and the passivity of the human interaction with computers that these hypermasculine cyborgs resist.

In *Terminator 2* the two metaphors for technology, one solid and the other fluid, explicitly do battle, thereby implicitly contrasting the metaphors attached to male and female bodies in the two-sex model. The new, more advanced terminator, the T-1000, is smaller than Arnold Schwarzenegger's original model 101 and does not have his immense physical strength. Instead, the T-1000 has the ability to transform himself into a stream of silvery liquid, and he can fashion himself into any shape, squeeze through tiny openings, and absorb punches and projectiles by molding himself around them, leaving holes where he once was. He is the embodiment of "feminine" fluidity, and as such is a particularly frightening adversary for the 101, since he does not fight in conventionally masculine ways. More important, he represents the loss of bodily boundaries that the 101 maintains with layers of leather clothing, big guns, and motorcycles. The film gives its allegiance to the solid 101, who is now a benevolent paternal figure who has traveled back through time to protect Sarah Connor's son John from the T-1000, who is on a mission to kill John. The 101 emerges victorious, proving the superiority of his solid masculinity by throwing the T-1000 into a giant vat of molten steel. Nevertheless, even the 101 is vulnerable to feminine bodies of water that are sufficiently deep and hot: he sacrifices himself in the same vat of molten steel to ensure that his advanced technology from the future will not be used in the present to increase the destructive power of machines. In his analysis of how the battle between the two terminators evokes a conflict between the sexes, Mark Dery writes that even while they die, the terminators display stereotypical male and female behavior: "In the movie's final moments, both Terminators are consumed in a vat of molten steel, where their mettle is revealed: The technetronic Teuton, Schwarzenegger, slips into the boiling goop with a chivalric wave of the hand worthy of a Wagnerian hero; the T-1000 squirms and shimmies, mouthing silent Edvard Munch–like screams in a most unmanly fashion."[30]

These cyborg films, however, do not always offer up a single unified

FIG. 18. T-1000 turns himself into silvery liquid in the
film *Terminator 2: Judgment Day.*

reading in support of a violently masculine position. In fact, they generally present conflicting tendencies, with narratives that often privilege
strong and autonomous women characters. What results is a clash of
protofascist masculine imagery with feminist ideals, often in the same
films. *RoboCop* presents a tough, resilient woman character, Anne Lewis,
who was policeman Alex J. Murphy's partner and becomes RoboCop's
sole ally. *The Terminator* pits the Terminator against Sarah Connor, an
unassuming college student and waitress who becomes tremendously resilient and resourceful and finally triumphs when she single-handedly
destroys the Terminator. Although her role in the future described by
Kyle Reese consists of motherhood, which resonates in the film with patriarchal Christian reverence (Sarah Connor is destined to give birth to a
son, John, who will become humanity's savior by leading a successful
revolt against the tyrannical machines), she is fated to be not a traditional
mother but a militaristic one who trains her son to become a skilled fighter
and leader. Indeed, in *Terminator 2* Sarah Connor has become a hard-

ened killer, closer in spirit to a machine than to the traditional concept of a nurturing mother. Her strength and lean, muscular physique can be appealing as a feminist alternative to helpless Hollywood women characters, but they also represent a misogynistic rejection of all things feminine. As Mark Dery writes, "All that flabby femininity has been flensed away like so much blubber."[31]

A single unified reading is especially difficult for the film *Eve of Destruction*. Its cyborg is a woman, Eve 8, who combines high-tech devices with genetically engineered organic parts and, most important, has a human psychological makeup. Eve 8 is programmed with the thoughts, feelings, and memories of scientist Eve Simmons. Even though *Eve of Destruction* gives us a female cyborg, it continues a misogynistic tradition, exemplified by *Metropolis*, of associating technology with women's bodies to represent the threat of unleashed female sexuality.[32]

Eve of Destruction shows that even when a film incorporates feminine metaphors for electronic technology, it can still enunciate a misogynistic position. The film combines electronic imagery from the late twentieth century with the industrial imagery of *Metropolis* to condemn female sexuality. Sexual difference is introduced early as a major theme of the film when the young son of Eve Simmons points to outlines of a nude man and woman in a children's book and announces to his mother: "This is a man. This is a woman. This is a vagina." He also identifies the figures' "tits" and "balls."

The film extends the child's anatomical lesson to create fear of what lies hidden deep within female bodies. Eve 8's body represents both steely industrial strength and the hidden mysteries of microelectronic circuitry. She is a fetishized phallic woman, but unlike her male counterparts RoboCop and the Terminator, her internal workings are even more dangerous than her muscular exterior. Eve 8's greatest threat lies deep inside of her womb, where the Defense Department has installed a nuclear bomb in order to use her as the ultimate weapon. Unlike the male cyborgs RoboCop, Doug Quaid, and the Terminator, Eve 8's threat is explicitly sexual; all her victims are men, and she frequently uses her body seduc-

FIG. 19. The female cyborg Eve 8 from the film *Eve of Destruction.*

tively to lure them. The film thus uses Eve 8's body to make a series of associations: female sexuality is linked to massive destruction in the misogynistic tradition of *Metropolis*, and both are associated with the inner workings of electronic technology. As if to emphasize the metaphoric connection between Eve 8's body and electronic technology, the film uses computer graphics to show how the tunnel inside her leads to the deadly nuclear device. Eve 8 evokes patriarchal fascination with and fear of that which is concealed and mysterious.

The film's narrative also combines fascination with fear and cannot entirely contain its cyborg once she has been set loose. In fact, the film can be read as a feminist revenge fantasy until the end, when a recuperative closure reestablishes patriarchal order by suppressing the woman's anger the film had previously unleashed. Because of its ending, the film cannot be characterized as feminist.

Eve of Destruction revolves around Eve Simmons, the scientist who created the cyborg Eve 8. The scientist and the cyborg not only share the

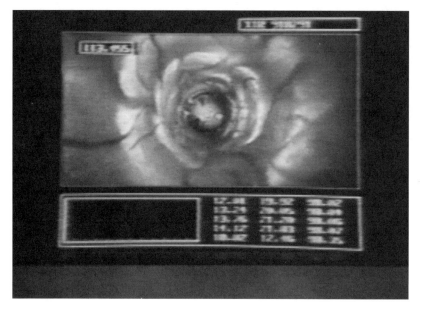

FIG. 20. A computer displays the tunnel leading to a
nuclear bomb in Eve 8's womb in the film *Eve of
Destruction.*

same memories but also look identical. When hit by gunfire during a test
run in the city, Eve 8 breaks away from her creators and goes on a rampage
that involves living out Eve Simmons's repressed fantasies of sex and revenge. To determine where Eve 8 will strike next, Eve Simmons must reveal to the military officer in charge of hunting Eve 8 her own private
thoughts, including sexual fantasies she had as an adolescent, revealing
the film's fascination with women's hidden psychological depth that corresponds to its concern with the concealed depths of electronic technology.

The film suggests that what emerges from women's deeply repressed
feelings is anger; Eve 8's rampage explicitly targets perpetrators of patriarchal abuse. Among the men killed by Eve 8 is Eve Simmons's father,
whose abusive rage had traumatized her when she was a child and who
had caused her mother's death. For days Eve 8's incredible rage and
strength allow her to resist the combined efforts of the police and the U.S.
military to capture and subdue her. It is Eve Simmons who finally kills

Eve 8 in a struggle for possession of Simmons's young son. Overturning the earlier feminist implications of the film, Eve Simmons ensures the preservation of patriarchal order by denying her own repressed rage and choosing her male biological child over her female technological creation. Nonetheless, the recuperative closure cannot entirely dispel the film's forceful representation of an angry female figure successfully taking on the forces of patriarchal oppression.

Not only does cyborg imagery in films extol the human killing machine, it also expresses the concomitant fear of sexuality discussed by Theweleit. In the film *Hardware* (Stanley 1990) the cyborg is dormant until it is activated by the sight of a young woman, Jill, having sex with her boyfriend. After the boyfriend has left the apartment, and Jill has hung the cyborg on the wall as part of a scrap metal sculpture, the cyborg watches her sleeping body for a while and then emerges from the wall to attack her—for like the Terminator, it has been created to destroy humans.

Fear of female sexuality also appears in non-Western cyborg texts. It dominates the low-budget Japanese cyborg film *Tetsuo: The Iron Man* (Tsukamoto 1989), a nightmarish vision in which a young businessman is transformed by machinelike appendages erupting from his body. He is simultaneously pursued by cybernetic creatures intent on merging with his body. The film's misogyny is as stark as its black-and-white images. Women attract and repel the protagonist; one performs an erotic dance, beckoning him with seductive gestures, and then sprouts a long snakelike metal phallus with which she rapes him. When he has sex with another woman, a giant electric drill erupts from his crotch and bores into her, causing her death. In *Tetsuo II: The Body Hammer* (Tsukamoto 1991) a man's murderous rage is explained in part by his boyhood observation of his parents having sex, an act that the film infuses with violence: his father holds a gun in his mother's mouth and shoots her. The boy then guns down both parents, using the skills he learned from his father, who created him to become a human weapon. He subsequently loses all memory of his childhood and the murders. As an adult, he is a meek weakling until pushed too far by a brute who murders his young son. His rage causes an arsenal of guns to erupt from his chest, and he goes after his persecutors with a vengeance, culminating in a showdown with his younger brother, who also witnessed the parental sex act. The film's relentless violence revolves around hypermasculine bodies that have been transformed by weight training and, as the next step, technological prostheses that assume gargantuan proportions. In the film's logic the transformations are fueled by the repressed memory of the primal scene.

Sexuality is feared by the protofascist soldier not only because it signifies loss of personal boundaries, writes Theweleit, but also because sexuality evokes the creation of life, and the soldier is bent on destroying all signs of life before they can destroy him. According to Theweleit, pregnant women are treated with particular revulsion in the soldiers' rhetoric. Indeed, cyborgs in films are often determined to prevent birth. In *Hardware* the cyborg that kills all the life-forms it encounters is a secret weapon in the government's birth control program. As film scholar Cynthia Fuchs writes, "The film charts the usurpation of reproductive processes by ultramilitary technology and governmental genocide."[33] The Terminator, likewise, has been programmed to travel back through time to prevent the birth of John Connor.

Creation versus destruction of life is not only a central thematic concern but also a site of dispute in cyborg texts. The ability to engender life is divided between men and women and between humans and technology. Women are typically associated with biological reproduction, whereas men are involved in technological creation. Preoccupation with technology functions to replace femininity and sexuality in many science-fiction films. In an essay entitled "The Virginity of Astronauts" Vivian Sobchack writes that the science-fiction film genre's "primary and unconscious—or subtextual—thematic problem" centers on "the male desire to break free from biological dependence on the female as Mother and Other, and to mark the male self as separate and autonomous." Referring to the genre's male astronauts, she writes, "As if in training for the big game, they have rejected their biology and sexuality—pushed it from their minds and bodies to concentrate on the technology required to penetrate and impregnate not a woman, but the universe." Sobchack shows that although sci-ence-fiction films feature chaste technocratic astronauts and banish women to the margins (that is, if they are not covered in asexual spacesuits that obliterate signs of femininity), the films are rife with displaced and condensed references to sex and biological reproduction. Aliens, ma-chines, and mutants become the creepy, fecund signifiers of sexuality and procreation.[34]

In the film *Demon Seed* (Cammell 1977) a scientist creates an artifi-cial intelligence in a sophisticated computer laboratory where teams of specialists educate their artificial child. The scientist's wife, Susan, is a psychiatrist, part of a humanistic profession that opposes her husband's technophilia. She complains about his emotional coldness, illustrating how the film defines gender roles in stereotypical ways: men are scien-tific and aloof whereas women are humanistic and emotional.

Demon Seed reinforces its version of gender difference by taking for granted that the artificial intelligence, a form of pure consciousness, is male. Masculine subjectivity has entirely dispensed with the need for a body in this film, existing instead as bodiless intellect. The woman's role is even further confined when Susan is raped by the artificial intelli-gence, whose pure intellect is the antithesis of Susan's reduction to a reproductive organ. Since the intelligence has no physical form (its name is Proteus IV, after the Greek sea god capable of assuming different forms), it relies on a robot and a giant mutating geometric shape under its com-mand to rape Susan. Its orgasm is represented as a trip into the far reaches of the cosmos ("I'll show you things only I have seen," it tells her). Moti-vated by a desire to produce a child and thereby experience emotions and physical sensations, the intelligence attempts to take control over the reproductive process, vying with Susan's husband for power over cre-ation. When the film ends with the birth of the child conceived by the artificial intelligence and Susan, it does not resolve whether the cyborg child, a union of a disembodied intellect and a human woman, will be demonic or benign.

Men are also the creators of life in the film *Weird Science* (Hughes

1985), a throwback to *Metropolis* with its representation of an artificial woman who is designed to fulfill a male fantasy. Two unpopular high school boys program a computer to create their perfect woman, one assembled from fragmented body parts selected from *Playboy* magazine. Her role, like the robot's in *Metropolis*, at first appears to be sexual; the boys' first desire, for example, is to take a shower with her. Also consistent with *Metropolis*, her sexuality is too powerful for the boys, who are incapable of doing more than just kissing her. Unlike her counterpart in *Metropolis*, however, she takes on a big-sister role that involves instructing the boys in the finer points of talking to girls. Her guidance boosts their self-confidence and allows them to win over the two most popular high school girls.

The ambiguities and contradictions surrounding the issues of sexual difference and reproduction/destruction are part of what makes these films compelling. The films assert the invincibility of patriarchal power and simultaneously show evidence that this power is crumbling. Even the figure of the aggressive male cyborg contains within it its own undoing, for its masculine strength exists at the expense of its human identity, and its artificial components, as is the case with all technology, have no sex. Sexual identity in the films transcends the human body and becomes attached to technology, but it also threatens to disappear if scrutinized too closely. Contradictions abound, and once they have been set in motion, even narrative closure cannot resolve them.

The contradictions embodied by the invincible armored cyborg in films have not gone unnoticed outside the film medium. In a brilliant display of cyberpunk commenting on itself, the comic book *Hard Boiled* (written by Frank Miller, who also wrote the comic book series *RoboCop versus the Terminator*, *Ronin*, and *Elektra Assassin*, among many others, and wrote the story and coauthored the screenplay for *RoboCop 2*) parodies the figure of the violent cyborg, as well as cyberpunk's hard-boiled conventions.[35] In issue number 2, in an urban wasteland that is stunningly sleazy and drawn in minute and graphic detail, a paunchy man and a flabby woman, both middle-aged and both cyborgs, fight brutally.[36] They

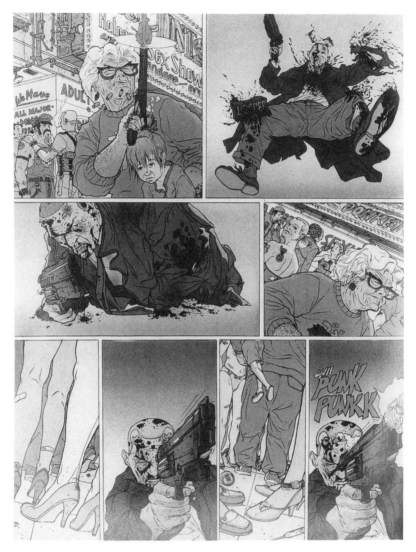

FIG. 21. Two middle-aged cyborgs try to destroy each
other in the comic book *Hard Boiled* number 2
(copyright © 1990 Frank Miller, Inc. and Geof Darrow.)

Fig. 22. Unit 4 is confused by the hardware in his body
in the comic book *Hard Boiled* number 2 (copyright ©
1990 Frank Miller, Inc. and Geof Darrow.)

crash their vehicles (cars with names like the Ford Stallone and the Eastwood), rip off each other's limbs, and punch grenades into each other's guts. Their assaults on each other destroy entire city blocks and kill hundreds of passersby, many of whom are already attacking and raping each other in the background. Meanwhile, the male cyborg, unit 4, tells himself in a terse monologue that he is, at different times, a tax collector named Nixon and an insurance investigator named, variously, Carl Seltz, Harry Seltz, Harry Burns, and Carl Burns. His monologue, which begins in issue number 1, combines hard-boiled clichés ("That's right. Come on. I got three bullets left") with clichés spoken by suburban fathers in 1960s television sitcoms: "Flapjacks and burgers. Becky makes it for me every morning and I never get sick of it. Some people complain about not having enough variety in their lives. Not me. I'm the kind of guy who likes familiar things. Watching the kids grow up. Driving my car. Seeing the same neighbors every morning. Everything familiar as my own name."

His own name, his neighborhood, and his wife and children (also cyborgs, unbeknownst to him) are all illusions created by the Willeford Home Appliances Company to convince him that he is human. Willeford's executives built him as an assassin to kill their corporate competitors. As if to dispel his growing doubts about himself, unit 4 frequently evokes his wife and kids in his monologues. At the end of issue 2 his flesh has been burnt away to reveal the metal structure inside, and he sits on the ground in a daze, saying, "What the heck's going on? I thought I was a normal guy! I can't go back to the wife and kids looking like this." As he staggers away in the last panel, an exit sign above him displays an arrow and the words "way out." *Hard Boiled* and the full spectrum of cyborg imagery thus tell us that the patriarchal system, with its brutal violence covered by sugary platitudes, is indeed on the way out, even if, in a last gasp, it has rallied its forces of muscular cyborg soldiers. At the end of the third and final issue of *Hard Boiled*, unit 4 has been rebuilt and reformatted by Willeford Home Appliances.[37] The last panel shows him kissing his wife after she greets him at the door of their home asking, "Bad day at the office?" His response, "No honey. Everything's fine," is wildly inappropriate given the day's events. The comic book provides a happy ending that deliberately shows the discrepancy between the myth of the perfect suburban family and the real social and technological upheavals of the postmodern late twentieth century. The world has changed, with power dispersing into bewildering networks of multinational corporations, which have their technological equivalents in the labyrinthine mazes of micro-circuitry.[38] Unit 4's insistence that he is a normal suburban father is as flimsy and doomed to fail as is the attempt to resist the changes of postmodernism by evoking nineteenth-century patriarchal and industrial strength with the figure of the seemingly invincible, armored, but ultimately self-defeating cyborg.

CHAPTER 5

Digital Rage

The tears
are long gone
and in their
place is
hardened
steel
desire.

Sarah, in *Hardwired*.[1]

EBATES RAGE IN THE POPULAR PRESS, as well as in specialized science and psychology texts, over whether computers can accurately simulate the human mind and, conversely, whether human minds are fundamentally computers. As Sherry Turkle writes, "One thing is certain: the riddle of mind, long a topic for philosophers, has taken on new urgency. Under pressure from the computer, the question of mind in relation to machine is becoming a central cultural preoccupation. It is becoming for us what sex was to the Victorians—threat and obsession, taboo and fascination."[2] So far computers themselves have not become active participants in the debate, although scholars have taken on the personae of computers to speculate on how history would be interpreted by an artificial intelligence tracing its own lineage.[3] But interest in the nature of the human mind has by no means displaced interest in sex. Within current discussions about the mind lingers the preoccupation with sex identified by Sherry Turkle as central to Victorian culture. Instead of existing as separate, distinct issues, thought and sex have become thoroughly entwined, even indistinguishable, in contemporary cybercultural discourses. Discussion of computation and reasoning in terms of sexual responses discursively erases the Cartesian separation between mind and body. Computers, it seems, have intensified, not diminished, our culture's fascination with sexuality. They have also prompted Hans Moravec to predict a future in which humans will lose their bodies and exist instead through software. In most fiction, however, computers have inspired flights of fantasy that remain firmly grounded in our current cultural preoccupations with sex and gender.

Ascription of sexuality to computers is part of a larger well-documented tendency for people to anthropomorphize computers.[4] Rochester and Gantz, in *The Naked Computer*, even refer to a computer's "excrement."[5] Humanlike computers have become commonplace in popular culture, with two of the most powerful examples occurring in the films *2001: A Space Odyssey* (Kubrick 1968), in which a spaceship's computer (HAL) becomes more emotional than the astronauts on board, and *Demon Seed*, discussed in chapter 4, in which an artificial intelligence rapes a woman psychologist. These films take anthropomorphism to an extreme, but computer functions do in some ways resemble human characteristics. Perhaps the most provocative similarity between humans and computers is memory. Anthropomorphism is implicit when we refer to a computer's memory, but the analogy has not been just a one-way street; researchers have turned it around to assert that human memory can be understood as a computerlike process of information storage and retrieval. Cognitive psychologists eager to solidify the analogy between humans and computers join AI researchers in arguing that human memory functions similarly to computer memory and that even the elusive human ability to create complicated associations can be reproduced by computers.[6] J. David Bolter responds to this way of thinking:

There is more to human memory than the ability
to repeat what is remembered. If men and women
are constantly forgetting what they learn, they
can also remember more than they learn. They
can trace out connections among sets of
disparate memories and not only on the aesthetic
level of Proust's associations on the scent of
madeleines. Memory, with its capacity to
establish structures of associations, is closely tied
to other faculties of reasoned thought and
creativity. It is in this sense that we live in the
world we remember, and it is this mysterious
capacity that psychologists and artificial
intelligence specialists would like to co-opt for
their computerized intellect.[7]

Despite the complexity of human memory, the model of a computer-mind has for some psychologists replaced the Freudian paradigm of layered levels of consciousness engaged in a process of repression. "The computer takes up where psychoanalysis left off," writes Sherry Turkle in her critique of the tendency to identify the human mind with computers.[8] The notion of a depthless self is one characteristic of what J. David Bolter calls "Turing's Man," the late-twentieth-century human defined as a computerlike artifact. Bolter writes that "the goal of artificial intelligence is to demonstrate that man is all surface, that there is nothing dark or mysterious in the human condition, nothing that cannot be lit by the even light of operational analysis."[9] As if to illustrate Bolter's observation, Roger C. Schank, who has written extensively on the parallels between computers and human minds, states, "we have seen that creativity, that mystical process known only to humans, is not really so mystical after all, and that it may well be possible to replicate creative behavior on a machine by transforming standard explanation patterns. From this it follows that the processes of creativity and learning are not so elusive, and may be quite algorithmic in nature after all."[10]

The appeal of computer existence for humans in the late twentieth century cannot be separated from the cultural crises confronting us, particularly the crises surrounding issues of sex and death. As discussed earlier, computer sex can pose an attractive alternative when physical sex carries the risk of AIDS. Computers have already become all-consuming for young men who perpetuate the caricature of the solitary social misfit who prefers to commune with his terminal rather than with people, especially women. A retreat from sexual involvement is evident in references to "the new celibacy" that crop up in the news media on a regular basis. Fantasies of solitary and cerebral machine sex are not entirely irrational given the new fear of physical sex. AIDS has also created an increased public awareness of human vulnerability and mortality. In a world where human bodies appear to be expendable, discourses of death, what journalist Frank Rich calls "the new blood culture," have become widespread. Rich explains the popularity of the film *Bram Stoker's Dracula* (Coppola 1992), Madonna's book *Sex*, and the vampire novels of Anne Rice as part of a larger "national psychic obsession" with the threat of death from infected blood.[11]

After a long Western cultural tradition of associating sex with death, sex is being replaced by computer use, which provides the deathlike loss of self once associated with sexual pleasure. Identifying with computers can be appealing on several levels in our fragmented postmodern existence. Vulnerable late-twentieth-century bodies and minds turn to electronic technology to protect themselves from confusion and pain. Fusion with computers can provide an illusory sense of personal wholeness; the fused cyborg condition erases the difference between self and other. Additionally, a wholesale embrace of computerized existence can create a sense that one's messy emotions have been replaced by pure logic and rationality. For those unable to cope with the complexity of human emotions, it might seem preferable to replace feelings with a limited repertory of automatic responses. For example, using a robotic, fortified self, the computer-human exemplified by RoboCop and the Terminator defends against both internal and external threats of dissolution.

Donna Haraway argues that cyborg existence need not be defined exclusively in terms of a fortified masculinist self, even though the Defense Department's prominent role in the development of cybernetic equipment has given the cyborg an aggressive military background.[12] Haraway proposes an alternative way of conceptualizing cyborgs in terms of a hybrid subjectivity. Her cyborg would adopt partial and contradictory identities that accept difference rather than defend against it. Although Haraway's hybrid cyborg is a far cry from the aggressive fortified cyborg, both visions suggest an idealized state of computer existence that rectifies the inadequacies and injustices of contemporary human life. The idea of a feminist cyborg, like the idea of a militaristic cyborg, arises from dissatisfaction with current social and economic relations, but the two cyborg visions offer vastly different solutions to our social ills.

The computer scientists who advocate downloading human consciousness argue that humans would achieve immortality, but the notion can also be understood to foretell human extinction. Human bodies are entirely expendable for these scientists. Speculation about the nature of human identity inevitably arises in discussions of human software copies. Computer scientists and science-fiction writers have speculated on the authenticity of electronically copied minds. The scientists, however, write from a strictly empirical standpoint using rhetoric that lends their exterminatory ideas the illusion of scientific validity. Marvin Minsky entertains the notion that a person's mind could be duplicated by creating a special computer chip for each brain cell. Minsky asks whether that new machine would be the same as the original if it were placed in the same environment and could function using the same processes as the original brain. He responds that microscopic differences would exist between the organic brain and the brain machine, since "it would be impractical to duplicate, with absolute fidelity, all the interactions in a brain." But you could not claim, writes Minsky, that these microscopic differences make the duplicate different from the original, for it, too, is constantly changing and will never be exactly the same as it was a moment before.[13]

Although Minsky's perspective is completely literal rather than metaphorical, his description of human identities undergoing constant changes resembles poststructuralist theories of decentered subjectivity, according to which individuals do not have fixed, stable identities but assume changing subject positions determined by language, gender, and other social and cultural institutions. He differs from poststructuralists in his faith in science. Minsky analyzes human identity to support his position that AI research, using the logic and rationality of science, can succeed in creating a computer equivalent to the human mind. For poststructuralist theorists, science, like any metanarrative that purports to express universal truths, is constrained by its ideological underpinnings and maintains its status as truth only within the confines of its own terms.[14] The case against scientific empiricism has in some cases been overstated, but Minsky's often inflammatory statements go a long way in blurring the boundary between science and science fiction.

Minsky's brain machine belongs to a future in which even human beings have been replaced by simulations: copies without originals. What Jean Baudrillard describes as our postmodern obsession with simulacra finds full expression in a world populated by electronically copied human minds.[15] Hans Moravec is even more unequivocal than Minsky in describing a future of mind simulation and human extinction. For Moravec, there would be no significant difference between the identity of an original mind and its copy except that the software copy would supplement the original personality with many new abilities. Humans, according to Moravec's misanthropic plan, should consent to their own extinction and cede the future to their computerized progeny.[16]

Cyberpunk fiction's visions of the future extrapolate from our current cultural preoccupation with computers to create worlds where the computer metaphor for human existence has triumphed. When cyberpunk characters are surgically hardwired, jack into cyberspace, load software directly into their brains, create computerized virtual bodies for themselves while their physical bodies decay, or abandon their bodies to exist inside the computer matrix, the boundary between human and computer is erased and the nature of the human psyche is redefined in accordance with the computer paradigm. Computers and human minds become thoroughly compatible because the differences between them have been effaced.

In cyberpunk and in some earlier science-fiction precursors, human mental processes are configured to function according to a digital model, allowing personalities and thoughts to be electronically coded and copied. Digital existence is a central aspect of George Alec Effinger's cyberpunk trilogy *When Gravity Fails, A Fire in the Sun,* and *The Exile Kiss.*[17] Characters acquire new personalities from the software modules they plug into their brains. Although most of the personalities in the modules are fictional characters, it is possible to create moddies from the mind of a living person, as the protagonist, Marid Audran, learns when a ruthless crime boss tortures him mercilessly and simultaneously records a moddie of his thoughts and feelings while he suffers. Audran refers to the experience as mind-rape, but he also concedes that Islam (the novels are set in the Middle East) will have to come to grips with the legal implications of personality modules recorded from living people, "just as the faith has had to deal with every other technological advance."[18]

The idea of digitally recording human minds finds expression in other cyberpunk texts as well. When characters in William Gibson's trilogy jack into simstim, they share the consciousnesses of simstim stars, whose experiences and feelings are recorded and transmitted directly into the minds of the public. A simstim link allows Case, the protagonist in *Neuromancer,* to vicariously experience the point of view and thoughts of his partner, the razorgirl Molly, when she stalks into dangerous situations.[19]

In both Gibson's and Effinger's novels the experience of plugging into another mind is often associated with sexual pleasure. Gibson's characters enter the pleasurable and exciting world of simstim to escape their

own dreary lives. In Effinger's *When Gravity Fails* Marid Audran is proposi-
tioned by Chiri, a bartender, who offers to plug in her new Honey Pilar
sex kitten personality module for him: "It was a very tempting sugges-
tion . . . with Honey Pilar's personality module plugged in, Chiri would
become Honey Pilar. She'd jam the way Honey had jammed when the
module was recorded. You close your eyes and you're in bed with the
most desirable woman in the world, and the only man she wants is you,
begging for you."[20]

Even though Marid initially resists getting his brain wired for personality modules because he is afraid of the way they "crammed you away in
some little tin box inside your head, and someone you didn't know took
over your mind and body,"[21] after he is forced to undergo the surgical
procedure, he takes pleasure in experimenting with a variety of modules.
And pleasure comes in all forms; for the powerful crime lord Shaykh Reda
Abu Adil, who tortures Marid, it means entering "Proxy Hell," chipping
in bootleg black-market moddies recorded from people experiencing the
horrible pain and suffering of torture or disease.[22] Effinger extrapolates
from the current tendency to associate computers with sex to create a
world where new technologies are immediately adapted to provide sexual
pleasure in even its most extreme forms.

In cyberworlds where minds can be manipulated like computers,
memories operate according to an electronic model; they can be enhanced,
augmented, changed, or erased. Since memories form the foundation of
human identity, loss of memory is equivalent to loss of self. This raises the
question addressed by Minsky and Moravec of whether an electronic copy
of a human mind is the same as the original. The film *Blade Runner*
revolves around this question (although its artificial humans are genetically engineered rather than electronically copied) by having both its
human and replicant characters treasure their personal collections of
photographs, which are visual signifiers of memories. Rachael, the most
advanced replicant, believes she is human because she remembers her
childhood, until she learns that the memories have been implanted in
her and actually belong to her inventor's niece. The film erases conven-

tional distinctions between humans and their artificial copies not only by
having the replicants collect memories in human fashion but also by having them surpass humans in the emotional qualities of love and compassion. Thus it suggests that advanced technologies might be used to destroy human uniqueness. Gabriele Schwab refers to this as the "dark side
of a culture of cyborgs" and comments on its ironic aspect: "Technology,
meant to extend our organs and our senses or even to support our fantasms
of immortality and transcendence, seems to threaten what we wanted to
preserve by destroying us as the subjects we thought ourselves to be when
we took refuge in technological projects and dreams."[23]

Loss of self through technological replication is the theme of the short
story "Overdrawn at the Memory Bank," written by science-fiction author
John Varley in 1976, nearly a decade before the cyberpunk movement
began. In the story people routinely record their memories and personality on "multi-holo" so they can be resurrected after death by having the
recorded material installed in a clone body. As Varley's narrator explains,
however, the new person will not be identical to the one who died, since
the recorded memories will not be up-to-date. There will be a gap in
memory matching the interval since the last multi-holo recording was
made. Varley writes, "A lot can happen in twenty years. The person in the
new clone body might have to cope with a child he or she had never seen,
a new spouse or the shattering news that his or her employment was now
the function of a machine."[24]

Varley's story explores a man's psychological trauma when he cannot
determine whether he and his world are real or computerized simulations. Synthetic existence is frightening in part because it confronts us
directly with unanswerable questions about our "authentic" lives. The
main character, Fingal, loses himself when he takes a virtual vacation by
having his personality recorded and installed in a lion roaming the artificial plains of "the Kenya disneyland." While he is experiencing life as a
lion, the technicians misplace his human body, so he returns to his own
consciousness inside a computer where his memories are being stored.
Inside the computer Fingal's life seems to proceed normally, except that

he is unable to determine whether he is really in a computer or is insane and suffering from delusions. What is worse, he realizes that it never has been possible to distinguish reality from illusion with absolute certainty and that the best people can do is "accept at some point what we see and are told, and live by a set of untested and untestable assumptions."[25]

In her novel *Mindplayers* author Pat Cadigan envisions a society where minds are routinely entered and copied.[26] Those who are dissatisfied with their lives can abandon their identities and buy a franchised personality sold by a company called Power People. One desperate character sells bootleg copies of his own personality. Others hire mindplayers to enter their minds via electronic hookups to their optical nerves (after temporarily removing their eyes) to explore their thoughts or introduce new mental material. When minds are routinely entered and duplicated, there ceases to be any concept of an authentic self and individual rights are threatened. In *Mindplayers* mindplay is controlled by the state and private corporations, and anyone the Brain Police catch indulging in illegal mindplaying activity could be sentenced to a mindsuck, which totally erases the identity and leaves an empty shell to be filled with a new state-sanctioned personality.

Computerized mind invasion also occurs in Walter Jon Williams's *Hardwired*, where a program called Project Black Mind "sets up a mind in crystal. Then goes into another mind, a live mind, and prints the first mind on top of it. Imposes the first personality on the second. Backs up the program."[27] The invaded mind is completely obliterated and replaced, leaving no trace of the original identity or personality. At the end of the novel Project Black Mind is used by Reno, who has lost his body and is trapped in the computer system, to invade the mind of Roon, an unscrupulous and powerful corporate director who takes orphaned children into his home and rapes them not only physically but also mentally: "he's studding himself into their brains so they can't get away from him, not even into their own heads."[28] Reno writes his own identity over Roon's mind with Project Black Mind, destroying Roon with suitable justice by using mind-altering techniques that Roon used relentlessly on his captive children.

Even though digital existence has taken hold in cyberpunk, humans have not been mindsucked into oblivion on a grand scale in these texts; they continue to experience the turbulent emotions and memories associated with earlier models of the mind. The desires and fears that Freud located in the human unconscious have not disappeared but continue to haunt cyberpunk characters. In fact, in fictional cyberworlds computer memory facilitates and even heightens the role that repressed emotions play in human and computer existence. Cyborgs are frequently troubled by emotional memories and are motivated by a desire for revenge in cyberpunk texts. Two of the best-known cyborgs whose actions are driven by repressed memories are RoboCop and Eve 8. Another haunted cyborg is Victor Stone, "a.k.a. Cyborg," in the comic book *Tales of the New Teen Titans.*[29] Stone is transformed from a black teenager into a part-machine, part-human steel-smashing titan with computerized components, but he continues to be aware of racial divisions in society.

When cyberpunk texts incorporate repressed memories, they often raise controversial social issues (as in the case of Victor Stone's experiences with racism), for a larger cultural context informs the cyborg's personal memories. One scenario that has emerged with remarkable frequency in cyberpunk is that of the cybernetic woman who seeks revenge for the emotional and sexual abuse she suffered as a child or young woman. She is simultaneously one of the most compelling and one of the most problematic figures in cyberpunk, for her appeal on a feminist level is frequently undermined by her conventional patriarchal presentation. Her ambiguous status has inspired contradictory interpretations and has sparked debates among commentators on cyberpunk. For example, Timothy Leary praises William Gibson's female characters, whom he calls "strong, independent, effective . . . heroic."[30] In contrast, Nicola Nixon asserts that cyberpunk's strong female characters "are effectively depoliticized and sapped of any revolutionary energy."[31] Nixon reads cyberpunk's version of strong, angry women as pale imitations of their feminist forerunners from the 1970s. In response to Nixon, John J. Pierce objects to what he calls her condemnation of "an entire subgenre as inherently sexist and reactionary."[32] Their exchange and the opinions of others on the same subject emphasize the ambiguity of cyberpunk's angry woman and her ability to evoke multiple and even contradictory responses.

The prototype for cyberpunk's angry cybernetically enhanced survivor of patriarchal abuse is Molly Millions from William Gibson's short story "Johnny Mnemonic"[33] and the novels *Neuromancer* and *Mona Lisa Overdrive*. Molly paid for her transformation into a sleek killing machine with money earned while working as a prostitute, where she experienced overwhelming depravity, including men killing women for sexual pleasure. When Case first encounters Molly in *Neuromancer*, she is wearing "tight black gloveleather jeans and a bulky black jacket cut from some matte fabric that seemed to absorb light." What he at first thought were her mirrored glasses on closer inspection turn out to be surgically inset mirrors "sealing her sockets. The silver lenses seemed to grow from smooth pale skin above her cheekbones." Case learns the extent of her surgical transformation when she says,

"you try to fuck around with me, you'll be taking one of the stupidest chances of your whole life."

She held out her hands, palms up, the white fingers slightly spread, and with a barely audible click, ten double-edged, four-centimeter scalpel blades slid from their housings beneath the burgundy nails.

Not only are her fingers switchblades, but her nervous system has been augmented with circuitry that gives her the "reflexes to go with the gear."[34]

Andrew Ross traces Molly's influence from Elektra in the comic book series *Elektra Assassin* to Abhor in Kathy Acker's novel *Empire of the Senseless*. "Both characters," Ross writes, "are steely, orphanesque survivors of a history of victimage that includes paternal rape, followed by repeated sexual predation on the part of violent males."[35] Indeed, the Ninja warrior-for-hire Elektra is filled with rage and has an unlimited capacity for violence after a childhood of paternal abuse.[36] The part-robot and part-black Abhor, who was also raped by her father, lives the violent life of an outcast.[37]

Fig. 23. Elektra Natchios, aka Elektra Assassin
(copyright © 1995 Marvel Entertainment Group, Inc.
Used with permission).

Acker's novel draws on cyberpunk imagery to rebel against patriarchal discourses, repeatedly revealing the violence and hatred that underlie them.

Yet another example of a cybernetic assassin is Sarah in Walter Jon Williams's novel *Hardwired*. As a child she was continually beaten by her father, and like Molly Millions, she earned money through prostitution to finance her independence and surgical transformation into a techno-killer. With her nervous system electronically hardwired to heighten her reflexes and allow her to interface directly with her weapons, and with a very tall and muscular body, she is a formidable opponent. Her internal weaponry takes the form of a "cybersnake," which she calls Weasel, that rises from her chest through her throat and out her mouth to attack her victims. A phallic serpent, it lies dormant until needed and then whips out like a killer erection. As Sarah explains, "the tears are long gone and in their place is hardened steel desire."[38]

The influence of Molly Millions can also be seen in the comic book series *Seraphim*, which follows the adventures of two cybernetically enhanced women warriors, Elle and Shinano, who work as assassins for the Autonomous Agency for the Enforcement of Humanity in A.D. 2095.[39] Finally, the comic book series *RoboCop versus the Terminator* spoofs both the RoboCop and Terminator films by having a tough woman fighter from the future named Florence travel back through time to kill Alex Murphy, the cop who is reconstructed as RoboCop in the RoboCop films.[40]

It is the premise of *RoboCop versus the Terminator* that the creation of RoboCop instigates computer sentience and ultimately leads to technology's catastrophic revolt against humanity. Although the warrior Florence is not a cyborg, she is a streamlined killer along the lines of Molly Millions and Elektra Assassin (also a Frank Miller creation) who takes on armies of terminators single-handedly.

Molly, Sarah, and the other hardwired women they have influenced clearly embody a fetishized male fantasy, but they also represent feminist rebellion against a brutal patriarchal system. It is difficult to either condemn or celebrate them, since a single interpretation cannot entirely explain their appeal. The same construction of multiple and contradictory readings occurs in films. In *Eve of Destruction* Eve 8 plays out a feminist fantasy when she methodically stalks and kills the men (and types of men) who abused her creator, scientist Eve Simmons, whose memories, thoughts, and feelings she shares. At the same time, however, the film condemns female sexuality and autonomy on a massive scale when we learn that Eve 8 contains in her womb a nuclear weapon on the verge of explosion and must be destroyed to save the planet.

Another ambiguous figure is Sarah Connor in the Terminator films, who transforms herself into a taut, muscular killing machine to prepare for the nuclear apocalypse and also as a reaction to the abuse inflicted on her by male doctors and attendants while she is imprisoned in a mental ward. Mark Dery points out with regard to Sarah Connor that "Hollywood's exploitation of the Freudian subtext of a sweaty woman squirting hot lead from a throbbing rod could hardly be called empowering."[41] Certainly Sarah Connor fits into a long tradition of phallic women in films whose fetishized bodies are designed to ease castration fears for the male spectator made uncomfortable by the sight of a fleshy woman on screen. Nonetheless, she also provides an attractive figure in the realm of fantasy for angry women. As viewers of martial arts films know, it is enormously satisfying to experience vicariously the triumph of an underdog seeking revenge against the perpetrators of injustice. Women under patriarchy can experience the exhilarating fantasy of immense physical strength and free-

Fig. 24. Sarah Connor is a hardened killer in the film
Terminator 2: Judgment Day.

dom from all constraints when watching figures like Sarah Connor. Revenge fantasies are powerful, even when they are packaged for consumption by the Hollywood film industry.

Because of the ambiguities and contradictions of her presentation, however, cyberpunk's figure of the angry woman can neither be hailed as a feminist paragon nor repudiated as a mere sex object; she incorporates aspects of both but fully embodies neither. In addition to her feminist potential, what is interesting about the hardwired woman is that she is motivated by human memories and emotions at all, for she has undergone a transformation from a human based on an organic model to one based on a computer model. After she has been remodeled, she abandons subtlety and indecision and instead reacts to events with the regularity and inevitability of a computer program. Whether she has been literally hardwired or not, her speed and decisiveness figure a computer's abilities. Her former passivity has been replaced with swift aggression. The transformation suggests that the only way to escape from victimization is to become a machine. Autonomy and strength, the texts tell us, derive from embracing a computerlike existence, for life as a human, especially as a woman, has become unbearable.

Most cybernetic women in cyberpunk, however, fail to give us a radically nonhuman vision of computerized existence. Repressed human memories and heightened emotions continue to motivate these hardwired women even after they have redesigned themselves. Instead of escaping from their human predicaments and entering a liberated electronic realm, they become haunted and powerful killers. Computerized minds harden and fortify them rather than provide partial and fluid cyborg identities. Actual computer characteristics are in fact distorted by their characterizations. The physical passivity that human computer users adopt is recast as aggressive violence. As described earlier in this book, the miniaturization and subtlety of computers are refashioned into bulging muscles that more closely resemble the enormous size and force of industrial technology. Additionally, gender, instead of disappearing, is often heightened after cybernetic transformation, a point that is obvious in Hollywood representations of ultramale cyborgs like the Terminator and RoboCop.

Although our culture is indeed preoccupied with the notion of computerized minds, there is an inability to imagine a truly nonhuman future.[42] Even when cybernetic characters relinquish their physical forms to enter the computer matrix, they are still preoccupied with human concerns. Sex continues to flourish in fictional electronic worlds. In some cases even the complete loss of human form fails to produce a significant departure from human sexuality. For some observers, the perpetuation of human sexual difference and desire is essential for the success of disembodied forms of life. As I mention in chapter 2, Jean-François Lyotard writes that AI can succeed in producing thought only if it incorporates memory, gender, and sexual desire. He explains, "We need machines that suffer from the burden of their memory."[43] For Lyotard, the force that propels thought is the desire induced by gender difference.

Nowhere is the persistence of human identity and sexuality after metamorphosis into a computer more clear than in the novel *Lady El* by Jim

Starlin and Diana Graziunas, published in 1992.[44] It follows in the foot-steps of other texts about a victimized woman's transformation into a hardwired killer, only this time the woman loses all physical form and literally becomes a computer. As do other texts, the novel illustrates the problem faced by readers of cyberpunk who enjoy the figure of the cybernetic woman survivor but are troubled by the persistence of patriarchal myths that inform her presentation. Like most of cyberpunk's angry women, Lady El does not have the enlightened perspective of Donna Haraway's cyborg. Although the novel begins by embracing feminist principles as it follows a woman's rejection of victimization, it ends by enacting the familiar patriarchal myth of the destructive sexual woman. It suggests that gender and sexuality transcend death and disembodiment and, when combined with the enormous power of technology, lead to massive and uncontrollable destruction. If a woman escapes victimization, warns the novel, her autonomy and sexual independence can rage out of control and destroy the world.

Lady El is short for Lady Electric, who begins her life as a human being named Arlene Washington. As a young woman she is killed by a subway train in a freak accident. After her death her brain is donated to the secret Project Cyborg and linked to a computer system. In her new life she is a brain floating in a jar connected to increasingly sophisticated and powerful computers. Eventually she is linked to the most powerful computer in the world, the Pentagon's NORAD computer, putting her in charge of an immense amount of data and important decisions, including, as she puts it, "the button, the entire works for the strategic nuclear planning for the whole damn U.S. of A." (268).

The scientist in charge of the project, Walter Hillerman, is surprised to learn that Lady El retains the complete identity of Arlene Washington.[45] He has collected ten brains in jars for the initial experiment, all of which a lab assistant has named after professional wrestlers, emphasizing the discrepancy between their disembodied state and a wrestler's exaggerated physique. Even though Walter Hillerman initially rejects the notion that the brains retain their original identities, one of the three ways that each brain is labeled refers to its former identity: "an F or M for the brain's sex" (35). The novel posits that a person's sex is located in the brain and out-lives the loss of the body. There is biological determinism at work in the notion that a brain, or any disembodied organ, has a sexual identity, as if any single part of a body in isolation can be identified as male or female. Additionally, by labeling the brains according to their sex, the novel continues a patriarchal tradition of making an individual's sex the principal basis for identification.

Lady El brings to her new job the memory of the violence that men continually inflicted on her since she was a little girl. Her first-person narration concentrates on how her new status as a cyborg has released her from victimization and endowed her with immense powers. She began her life with, as she puts it, three strikes against her: she was poor, black, and female. Her childhood turned into a nightmare after her father died and her mother took in a violent and abusive man named Levar who continually raped the thirteen-year-old Arlene and then, a year later, started to sell her to his friends. Arlene finally ran away to New York and got a job on the night shift as a cleaning woman in the World Trade Center. She also began a series of degrading relationships with violent, drug-addicted or alcoholic men.

After Arlene's death and resurrection as Lady El, however, she realizes that in her former life she had been the victim of racism and had lived her life as an "emotional junkie" who always depended on a man to tell her what to do and think. Her new cyborg existence gives her perspective on her past life and allows her to become increasingly powerful as she is given access to enormous data banks and asked to make decisions of considerable importance. She enjoys lightning-speed learning from the data banks and expands her consciousness by sharing the memories of a white man's and a white woman's brains plugged into her system. Because of her new perspective, she adopts the motto "power = survival" (131) and soon after revises it to "knowledge + power = survival" (135).

She uses her new knowledge and power, however, in ways that continue, rather than reject, her concerns from the past. Even in the form of

an on-line brain, she has not abandoned the desire for love or the tendency to make men her first priority. Most of her time is spent obsessing
about Walter Hillerman. She tells the reader, "I'll 'fess up. I courted the
man. My every waking moment was spent on thinking how I could please
him" (178). What has changed is that, unlike Arlene Washington, she is
determined to maintain her power and is, as she puts it, "clearly developing an affection for men who could be controlled" (184). Her main liabil-
ity, as she sees it, is her lack of a body, so she secretly designs and builds a
robot body to occupy, one she describes as "every man's wet dream" (224).
Despite the fact that she has rejected the role of victim, she still changes
herself for a man, in this case literally building herself from scratch. Her
idea of power is to succeed by conforming to the system rather than opposing it; the robot body she designs is based on racist stereotypes of beauty.
She declares, "I wanted to be a blonde! A blue-eyed, blond California
beach baby! Barbie with a brain!" She continues, "I bet lotsa brothers and
sisters would be ready to jump on me 'bout my choice. Think I was a
traitor, ashamed of my race and all. But that wasn't it. Wasn't it at all.
Time as a computer had taught me to face facts. And one fact that couldn't
be ignored was that America's a racist society. Sure, it's got a lot of good
things goin' for it, but basically the status quo is that the whites got it and
the blacks don't" (223).

What Lady El discovers is that even after escaping racism with her
white robot body, she must still contend with sexism, and when she confronts an aggressive man, her new computer self acts quickly and deci-
sively: she kills him. Chuckie Baxter III, picked up by Lady El on a telephone party line, tries to force sex on her and ends up with his chest
impaled on her fist. Soon thereafter she designs another robot body, this
one a black woman, to visit and attack her childhood abuser, Levar, leaving him "scared, crippled, helpless, finally gettin' a taste of what it means
to be a victim" (256). Lady El is driven by revenge and anger, and her
violent attacks occur with sudden unstoppable force. As she says after
killing Chuckie, "I'd flipped out. That's what I'd done, plain and simple.
I'd blown my cork. Freaked out. Short-circuited. Gone crazy. Killed me a

not-so-innocent man. Killed him dead, all right. And all 'cause he was goin' to date rape me" (238). No longer a victim, she recognizes how far she has come: "I knew I was a dangerous weapon" (258).

The novel escalates her strength and turns her from an angry woman into a global tyrant when she is linked to the Pentagon's NORAD computer. She announces, "No one would ever be able to push Arlene Washington around again. 'Cause I'd just become the world's newest nuclear power" (270), "the most powerful and independent creature on the face of this good green earth" (283). Her dangerous strength erupts when Walter and a policeman figure out that she killed Chuckie Baxter; her immediate response is to kill the policeman. When Walter tries to destroy her, she confesses her love for him, and when that fails to stop him, she emerges in a new robot body—a naked red-headed woman—and kills Walter with a rod through his heart. She declares, "I wasn't in the mood to sacrifice myself for love" (304). After his death their roles reverse and she becomes the creator, removing his brain and linking it to a look-alike Walter automaton she has constructed. Her work is so successful that no one realizes that Walter has been killed and replaced by a robot. Lady El has achieved complete control over Walter, as well as over the computer world. At the end of the novel she has attained her dream: power and the man she loves. She announces to Walter, "This world of the computer will be our own little corner of paradise" (324).

The novel leaves the computerized Lady El resolutely human by making her driven by memories of abuse and obsessed with sexual desire. Like so many texts that perpetuate the patriarchal archetypes of virgin and vamp, *Lady El* warns that a powerful sexual woman poses a terrible threat. Transformation into a computer does nothing to change the spiderwoman archetype except to endow her with more massive powers than could ever be imagined by a film noir seductress. Even though the novel is fascinated by the idea of computerized existence, it regards the possibility of life as a computer with the simultaneous fear and hope that, after all, nothing will change.

Brooks Landon, author of wide-ranging analyses of science fiction and postmodernism, has written that cyberpunk fiction is destined to phase out after a relatively short time because its real message is *"inevitability—not what the future might hold, but the inevitable hold of the present over the future—what the future could not fail to be."*[46] The future drawn inevitably from our present is one in which profound ambivalence exists over the value of human identity, the nature of computerized existence, the transcendence of sexuality, the consequences of racism, and the persistence of gender. Sex, death, race, and gender issues infiltrate Lady El's little corner of cybernetic paradise just as they inhabit the visionary musings of anyone concerned with how the cultural tensions of today will unfold in the unpredictable worlds of tomorrow.

CHAPTER 6

Men and Machine-Women

I'm

the brains

and

the muscle.

Eve Edison,
in *Mann and Machine.*

M ANN AND MACHINE, an NBC television series that aired in the spring
of 1992, introduced a new fictional machine-woman named Eve
Edison, a sergeant in the Los Angeles Police Department in the
"near future." The series revolved around the crime-fighting adventures
of Eve and her police detective partner, Bobby Mann. An analysis of Eve
provides insight into how the figure of the mechanical woman has evolved
over the course of the twentieth century. Her evolution has been shaped
by the microelectronics revolution and equally revolutionary social
transformations, in particular, the rise of feminism and the spread of

postmodernism. These developments can be observed by comparing Eve to what is perhaps the best-known and most influential machine-woman from the early twentieth century, the robot Maria in *Metropolis*. Despite their shared combination of technology and female sexuality, however, Maria and Eve Edison are different kinds of mechanical women. Nonetheless, even though the late-twentieth-century Eve is a different sort of technological and cultural construct from the early-twentieth-century Maria, she exists in a text that, like *Metropolis*, conveys the same old misogynistic message about the dangers of female sexuality.

It is unclear whether Eve is an android or a cyborg. Eve's creator, Dr. Kepler, explains that Eve is not like other machines. Her brain is a "neural model," and she learns from experience, like humans. What is not clear is whether Eve's brain is made of biological neurons or artificial electronic imitations, but Dr. Kepler says that Eve could become human over time. If not a cyborg at present, then, she has the capacity to evolve into one.

As is often the case with science fiction, *Mann and Machine* gives us a vision of the future while drawing its inspiration from older texts, and in this case the result replays conventional patriarchal ways of thinking about men and women. This close analysis is based on the first four of the nine episodes of *Mann and Machine*. The series derived its narrative, characterizations, visual style, and musical score from a variety of sources that include the television program *Miami Vice*, the films *Blade Runner*, *RoboCop*, and *Eve of Destruction*, the hard-boiled detective genre, cyberpunk fiction and comic books, and a late-nineteenth-century French novel, *L'Eve future* (*Tomorrow's Eve*), about a mechanical woman.[1] It recycled and recombined their elements in a postmodern pastiche to arrive at its message about gender relations: a real man, Bobby Mann, requires a woman who is dependent on him, even if she surpasses him in intellectual and physical strength. To avoid making her insufferably dependent, however, the makers of *Mann and Machine* created an innocent young Lolita who was drop-dead gorgeous and had the survival skills of RoboCop.

Eve is a recent addition to a long line of sexy mechanical women in films and fiction. Her name recalls not only the biblical Eve but also the cyborg from the film *Eve of Destruction* and the novel *L'Eve future*, written by Villiers de l'Isle-Adam in 1886. In the novel the mechanical woman, named Hadaly, is built by inventor Thomas Edison in an attempt to create the perfect woman, a project that recalls the ancient Greek myth of Pygmalion and Galatea, as well as all the other tales, including the recent films *Weird Science* and *Cherry 2000*, of men trying to seize control over reproduction in order to fashion the ideal woman.

Annette Michelson argues that *L'Eve future* was written at a critical historical moment, the early 1880s, when mechanical reproduction was first introduced to the world in its earliest manifestations. The novel's interest in constructing an ideal woman intersects historically with the use of photographic reproduction to create the perfect female image, setting the stage for early cinema to unveil its obsessive fascination with the female form in the 1890s. Cinema, writes Michelson, is like Edison in Villiers's novel: it creates an idealized synthetic woman to tempt its beholders, who, despite their knowledge of the woman's artificiality, are completely dazzled and agree to accept and adore her as Woman.[2]

The name Eve Edison in *Mann and Machine* plays on *L'Eve future* by giving Eve her "father's" name, tracing her lineage back to the novel and the inventor. What becomes clear during the first four episodes is that Eve Edison is indeed under the patriarchal control implied by her last name, because even though she was created by a woman scientist, she learns about the world and human behavior from Bobby Mann. He makes a joke out of his desire to control Eve when he is introduced to her and says sarcastically, "This time I want the owner's manual." The scientists dutifully provide him with several thick volumes. To put it in Lacanian terms, Eve's entry into the symbolic order involves submitting to the authority of the father. In this respect she carries on the long-standing literary and cinematic tradition of female mechanical figures who are used to play out patriarchal notions about relations between the sexes.

A recent example of how mechanical women have been eroticized is the book *Sexy Robot* by Hajime Sorayama, a collection of drawings of metal-plated scantily clad or nude women posed like *Playboy* centerfolds. It includes step-by-step instructions on "how to draw the sexy robot." Sorayama writes by way of introduction, "The first idea I had for sexy robots was to try to combine robots and eroticism. The problem was where to leave a touch of the human—the lips, the breasts, the hips. And you have to make it look like they are going to move at any time now. That's why they're full of lies."[3]

Most of the bodies drawn by Sorayama are almost entirely robotic, with heads like motorcycle helmets, but they are voluptuous and often wear skimpy swimsuits that eroticize their hard metal surfaces. Their "lies," to use Sorayama's term, are actually similar to the lies expressed by all idealized and air-brushed centerfolds; whether they have flesh-colored skin or metallic silver bodies, they all look unreal. Sorayama's robots do not evoke the uncanny and disturbing sense that inanimate objects have taken on human life; rather, they appear familiar and conventional despite their metallic bodies.

Significantly, *Mann and Machine* introduces Eve through the eyes of Mann, whose predicament dominates the first episode. Mann represents not only the human condition in contrast to that of the mechanical Eve but also the particular condition of a man who is uncomfortable with women and the breakdown of traditional gender roles. Mann's response to women is summed up by the comment that the only female he can live with is his dog. His discomfort is exacerbated by the fact that he is surrounded by women in positions of power. During the first episode we learn that Mann reports to a tough-as-nails black woman captain, he is divorced, he sees his daughter only every other weekend, and he cannot get his favorite chocolate donuts out of a snack machine that speaks to him in a woman's voice. His anger explodes during the first scene of the episode when one of the few other men around, his robot partner before Eve joins the squad, launches into touchy-feely psychoanalysis in their squad car and then offers to give Mann a massage, receiving the homophobic reprimand, "If you touch me, I'll kill you." By immediately situating the viewer in Bobby Mann's misogynistic perspective, the series

FIG. 25. Detective Bobby Mann and his mechanical
partner Eve Edison in the television series *Mann and
Machine.*

establishes the premise that the machine-woman will be judged on the
basis of her relationship to him.

By establishing that Mann is unenthusiastic about both women and
machines, the series leads us to believe that there will be friction between
Mann and Eve. But Mann quickly discovers that Eve is a misogynist's
dream come true; although she looks like a full-grown voluptuous woman,
she knows nothing about the adult world of love and sex. As Dr. Anna
Kepler, the coolly efficient director of the AI program, tells Mann, even
though Eve is highly advanced intellectually, "in emotional terms she's
very young." When Mann insists on a rough estimate of just how young
Eve is in emotional terms, Dr. Kepler replies, "seven." "Perfect," says Mann,
with only a hint of sarcasm. *Mann and Machine* proceeds to maintain
that a man can find happiness with a childlike woman, even if the woman
is a machine.

The robot Maria in the film *Metropolis*, in contrast, is above all sexually aggressive and threatening. In his analysis of the film Andreas Huyssen argues that the robot represents both female sexuality and technology running out of control; she is an embodiment of early-twentieth-century male fear of women and machines.[4] Both women and machines were thought to possess powers that, if unleashed, could prove disastrous to patriarchal order. Indeed, Maria uses her sexuality to lead the downtrodden workers in a revolt against their capitalist masters, nearly causing the destruction (by flooding, which has a connotation of feminine fluidity) of both the workers' underground community and the soaring city of Metropolis above. Destruction is averted by burning the lascivious robot Maria at the stake and also, writes Huyssen, by diminishing the strength of the human Maria, whose body was the model for the robot and whose life force was drained and transferred to it. At the beginning of the film the human Maria is energetic and forceful, and Freder Fredersen, the son of the master of Metropolis, is captivated by her allure. By the end of the film, however, she is "a helpless mother figure who is totally dependent on male support."[5] The film leaves us with two archetypal constructions of femininity in the two Marias, the virgin and the vamp, and Huyssen writes that the same duality characterizes the film's attitude toward technology. Machines in the film are capable of either submissive obedience or uncontrollable force. The film's conflation of women and technology thus functions to evoke and then eliminate the dual threat of sexuality and technology. Patriarchal and capitalist order is restored by suppressing women and sexual desire and harnessing mechanical power.

In its vision of the future *Metropolis* depicts an absolutely patriarchal society. Industrialist Jon Fredersen (John Masterman in the English translation) possesses dictatorial rule over the city of Metropolis and its underground community of workers. His power extends over a highly stratified society where both class and gender roles are rigidly compartmentalized. The wealthy elite who benefit most from Fredersen's rule are all men; we see them at a party where the robot Maria performs an erotic striptease for their admiring gaze. Fredersen's closest associate in the film is the male inventor Rotwang, and in their collaboration we see science serving the

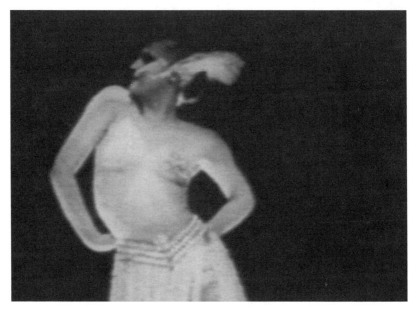

FIG. 26. The robot Maria makes her public debut by
dancing enticingly for a party of leering men in the film
Metropolis.

state, using its specialized knowledge to assist in the suppression of dis-
sent. The power of science and the state resides entirely in wealthy men
who use their strength to maintain control over women and working-class
men, who, it can be argued, have been feminized by their subordinate
position.

In *Mann and Machine* the vision of the future has changed. No longer
male dominated, the society in *Mann and Machine* depicts women in
positions of power in law enforcement and science. Detective Bobby Mann
reports to a woman, Captain Claghorn, and another woman, Dr. Kepler,
has supplied the specialized knowledge that makes possible a mechanical
police sergeant. Once again, science serves the state, but now both science
and the state are represented by women. The powerful women feared by
the ruling men of *Metropolis* are in control in *Mann and Machine*, and
Bobby Mann's brand of tough-guy masculinity is under siege. He responds
by wandering around with a perpetual sarcastic sneer that communicates

the world-weary disdain he shares with Rick Deckard in *Blade Runner* and all the other hard-boiled detectives who are their forerunners.

Another way to describe the future extrapolated from 1992 in *Mann and Machine* is to say that it is the product of postmodernism. For one thing, it was broadcast on television. In chapter 4 I argue that television exemplifies postmodern fragmentation and disruption, in contrast to film's more linear and coherent style of representation. In terms of its visual style, *Mann and Machine* epitomizes the slick, glossy postmodern look made popular by *Miami Vice* with its highly mediated surfaces, where color and texture take precedence over narrative progression. *Mann and Machine* bathes its images in blue and pink and an abundance of neon, which occasionally creates a sultry ambience heightened by a bluesy saxophone in the musical score but at other times functions merely as aesthetic flourish. Space in the series also follows the precepts of post-modernism; it consists of circuitous twists and turns, and the editing style creates highly ambiguous spatial relations between shots. This is the confusing use of space that Fredric Jameson identifies as the postmodern architectural equivalent to the logic of multinational capitalism.[6]

In contrast, spatial and social relations in *Metropolis* are more clearly delineated: the rich live on top of the poor, literally and figuratively. The city's wealthy class lives in lofty skyscrapers aboveground, while the work-ers exist underground, toiling in hellish machine rooms and living in squalid quarters located even lower under the ground. Although the city's spatial arrangement clearly duplicates its distribution of power, its layout is not entirely geometrical. Deep below the surface of the earth, lower even than the workers' dwellings, are the catacombs, and it is here, in a large cavern, that the human Maria preaches to the assembled workers. She holds sway over the workers in the cavern, standing radiantly before them. Moments later, however, after the crowd of workers has dispersed, Rotwang pursues Maria through the catacombs' winding tunnels, intent on capturing her to complete his robot in her likeness. Film scholar Roger Dadoun points out that these twisting paths leading through dark caverns create a feminized space, a metaphor for the womb, reinforcing the film's construction of Maria as a maternal figure and evoking female sexuality.[7] This feminized space exists far below the surface of the earth because, in psychoanalytic terms, female sexuality has been deeply repressed in the city of Metropolis. Up above, on the surface of the city and its ego, loom the powerful phallic skyscrapers. The narrative shows the eruption of female sexuality and its subsequent destruction, which the film deems necessary for the maintenance of order.

The subterranean feminized space of *Metropolis* has surfaced in *Mann and Machine*, where it pervades the Los Angeles of the near future. Space consists almost entirely of serpentine corridors and dimly lit rooms and back alleys. Even the police station presents a confusing layout of halls and offices, making it difficult to imagine how the parts connect. Between 1926 and 1992, then, there has been a reconceptualization of the future in terms of sex. *Metropolis* depicts men maintaining control over the repressed female realm. *Mann and Machine* represents beleaguered men surrounded by the ubiquitous presence of women and feminized space.

A transition from male to female dominance also extends to the depiction of technology in the two texts. Maria in *Metropolis* is made from steely hard industrial technology. Eve, however, is the product of electronic technology's microcircuitry. During the time that has elapsed between Maria and Eve, culture has been transformed. Electronic technology has become dominant and the industrial age has given way to the era of multinational capitalism and the ethos of postmodernism. Representations of industrial machines tended to concentrate on their sheer physical force, on the power of their pumping, grinding, and turning parts. When human bodies were represented as machines in modernist art, they too were identified on the basis of vigorous physical movement. Industrial-age machine-bodies tended to be associated with phallic power, whether they were pumped-up male superheroes or aggressive phallic women like the robot Maria in *Metropolis*. Nineteenth and early-twentieth-century patriarchy used the machine metaphor to fortify its sense of power; the machine as phallus declared men's invincible dominance over women. As Fredric Jameson explains, however, electronic technology no longer evokes the imagery of physical prowess; it functions more passively and quietly than industrial machines, and its workings are hidden behind the screen instead of being on display.[8] Industrial machines evoke masculine metaphors, whereas electronic technology no longer has the same powerful associations (see chap. 4). Donna Haraway writes, "Modern machines are quintessentially microelectronic devices: they are everywhere and they are invisible. Modern machinery is an irreverent upstart god, mocking the Father's ubiquity and spirituality."[9] Electronic technology can bring to mind feminine rather than masculine metaphors.

Even though electronic technology can evoke feminine metaphors in terms of its appearance and functioning, however, it is not at present feminist. Donna Haraway cautions that "miniaturization has turned out to be about power; small is not so much beautiful as pre-eminently dangerous, as in cruise missiles." She also writes that despite its mobility and portability, electronic technology causes "immense human pain in Detroit and Singapore."[10] What has become essential, argues Haraway, is for women to overcome technophobia and embrace new technologies. Only then will it be possible to overturn masculine systems of domination. Haraway's manifesto reveals how electronic technology can be described metaphorically as feminine and can even inspire feminist visions of the future. Her musings are an alternative to the RoboCop and Terminator films where, as I argue in chapter 4, technology is associated with industrial strength and serves primarily to reinforce masculine power.

Eve Edison, on the other hand, is associated with computers in *Mann and Machine*; she is an information specialist, a "retrieval expert" who jacks into the computer by inserting a plug in her ear. She explains, "my brain downloads directly into the computer." Once jacked in she can scan computer data and cross-reference files extremely quickly, speeding up the process of solving crimes. She is also capable of what she calls retinal scanning—popping in a new eyeball to read computer files even more quickly—and of replaying her stored visual memories. *Mann and Machine* celebrates her amazing microelectronic feats without exploring their insidious implications: Eve represents the potential for complete

FIG. 27. Eve Edison is jacked into the computer in the
television series *Mann and Machine.*

police surveillance over the public. The information age has already made
everyone vulnerable to computerized invasions of privacy. Eve shows how
even feminized technology can be used to institute systems of domination. When she jacks into the computer and scans voluminous amounts
of data in a matter of seconds, she takes to new extremes the omnipotence
of institutions with access to computer files.

Eve is not entirely passive, however; she also possesses extraordinary
physical strength and quick reflexes that come in handy when she and
Mann do battle with criminals. She combines industrial-age machine
strength with electronic-age computing skills, a combination that mirrors
the simultaneous presence of industrial machines and electronic technology in the late twentieth century.

Even though Eve is not a phallic threat, *Mann and Machine* does not
articulate a feminist position. It has not progressed beyond the age-old
idea of the danger posed by female sexuality. One episode involves a man
who runs a dating service and kills the women clients he finds attractive.

Another involves a woman who seduces young men and then kills them and sells their organs on the black market. In another a woman environmentalist turns out to be the sexy moll of a notorious criminal. She uses her job as a water purification expert to divert huge quantities of precious clean water to the criminal's wine import business. The message is the same as the one in *Metropolis*: sexuality is dangerous, and sexual women pose a threat either because they are killers themselves or because they incite violence in men.

In *Metropolis* unrestrained sexuality is embodied by the machine-woman. This also holds true for the film *Eve of Destruction*, which is in some ways a contemporary version of *Metropolis*, for the cyborg Eve represents the uncontrollable destructive force of women's unleashed desires. In *Mann and Machine*, however, the machine-woman no longer poses the threat. Eve Edison represents a controllable woman. The series uses a feminine metaphor for electronic technology merely to create another patriarchal stereotype. Eve's subordinate status is guaranteed by her naïveté; she has the developmental level of a child. Her creators sent her to a nursery school class to learn socialization skills, and as a result, her favorite book is *The Runaway Bunny* and she is enthusiastic about the game "Pin the Tail on the Donkey." In some respects, however, Eve is extremely intelligent; the series gets a lot of mileage out of the conventional opposition between machine reason and human emotion by playing Eve's rational mode of reasoning off of Mann's impulsive decisions. The series thus avoids the stereotypes of emotional women and rational men.

Ultimately, however, the power of Eve's rational mind is undermined by her ignorance. She knows nothing about conventional norms of adult human sexual behavior and the conventional social roles of men and women. Even though she has been programmed with great quantities of knowledge, she does not know how she is supposed to function as an adult woman. It is thus Bobby Mann's job to teach her, and the series revolves around his efforts. Some of Mann's coaching consists of introducing human disorder into Eve's carefully ordered machine life. He throws the clothes hanging neatly in her closet and her row of books all over her bedroom floor and tells her to leave a half-empty bottle of beer in her refrigerator and dirty dishes in the sink. She happily agrees, because she wants to be human. What we see, however, is yet another man forcing a woman to change for him, and when he yanks her clothes out of her closet and throws them on the floor, his actions have the connotation of male violence against women.

Mann is most insistent about teaching Eve that she should hide her body and her sexuality. In one case he tries awkwardly to explain to her that he gave her a low mark for modesty in his written evaluation of her because she should have closed the door when she changed her clothes. He is uncomfortable with her sexuality, especially when she wears revealing clothing or speaks frankly about sexual matters. Even though Eve's sexuality is childlike, she makes Mann squirm with discomfort. Between *Metropolis* and *Mann and Machine* the message remains the same: female sexuality is dangerous when it is allowed to surface.

Nevertheless, in the postmodern milieu of *Mann and Machine* everything is already on the surface; there is no longer the possibility of repression in this world of Baudrillardian simulations, where everything circulates in the open.[11] Indeed, Eve's innocent sexual openness resists Mann's efforts to subdue her. After Mann tries to teach Eve about the need for modesty, he tells her to leave his bathroom, where she has been watching him shave. He intends to disrobe and take a shower. She wants to stay and promises to close her eyes. After closing them briefly, however, she peeks and grins widely. She refuses to repress her curiosity about human bodies and sexuality. In another episode she and Mann go undercover to infiltrate the black market in human organs, posing as a married couple desperate to buy a testicle. Eve questions both Mann and Captain Claghorn about what she perceives as the peculiar significance for men of such a small organ. Her innocent wonder at social codes and taboos leaves her, at least to some extent, outside patriarchal control.

The gender politics of *Mann and Machine* thus fail to achieve a fully coherent patriarchal position, leaving room for feminist implications to emerge. Because Eve is shown in the process of becoming gendered, *Mann* and *Machine* can be read in a manner that exposes rather than fortifies patriarchal manipulation of women. Eve looks like an adult woman, but she does not always think or act in ways that patriarchy deems natural for adult women. Although she has a female body, her gender is not intrinsic to her form. Rather, it is added to her mental program step by step as she learns from Mann and her environment. The series thus exhibits the social construction of gender: Eve is taught how to be a woman; it does not come naturally to her.

When Mann explains to Eve why he gave her a low mark for modesty, the tension between biological and cultural explanations for gender roles comes to the forefront. After Mann extols the virtues of modesty, the two have the following conversation:

EVE: *What's the logic on that?*

MANN: *The logic? I'm a man; you're a woman.*

EVE: *Technically not true.*

MANN: *Well you look like one. And to a man the sight of a naked female body is . . .*

EVE: *A negative?*

MANN: *No, it's beautiful, but distracting.*

Eve's comment that she is technically not a woman can be understood in two ways: on the one hand she is saying that she is a machine and therefore does not have a sex, and on the other hand she could be implying that the notion of "woman" is a social construct even for human beings and that sexual difference does not necessarily result in behavior that falls neatly into the gender categories "man" and "woman." Mann's response suggests that the truth is irrelevant to him; as long as something looks like female sexuality, no matter what it is, it should be hidden. As long as Eve looks female, he tells us, she will "distract" men, and therefore she must adopt the modesty assigned to women under patriarchy.

What Mann says to Eve about appearances being more important than the truth ("you look like one") extends to the position taken by *Mann and Machine* as a whole. The series depicts a culture in the near future no longer characterized by the conditions that reinforced patriarchal control during the nineteenth and early twentieth centuries. Women have achieved positions of power in the work force, systems of social control have become more complex, and technology no longer fortifies phallic dominance. These conditions are to some extent accurate reflections of present-day culture in the United States, although women's entry into the work force in large numbers has not yet brought them many positions of power in the upper echelons of business, politics, science, or law enforcement. At the same time that it represents social changes, however, the series takes the position that they are irrelevant. It maintains that no matter how much evidence exists that women are not naturally inferior to or dependent on men, sex roles should continue to follow patriarchal dictates. Even though the series exposes patriarchy as a culturally imposed set of rules, it still upholds those rules.

Mann and Machine thus illustrates a textual practice of supporting a dominant ideology without trying to justify or naturalize it on the basis of any "truth." The series is evidence that patriarchal ideology tenaciously persists in the late twentieth century despite all the cultural changes that reveal its artificiality. Even so, *Mann and Machine* may indicate that patriarchal ideology is unraveling. No longer coherent in its textual presentation, patriarchal ideology persists amid glaring contradictions and tensions. The opportunity to watch *Mann and Machine* develop the tensions it set in motion around men, machines, and women did not exist, since the series was canceled after one season. Whatever the reason for its cancellation, *Mann and Machine* has given us a glimpse of how the machine-woman metaphor can function in the waning years of the twentieth century, when the changes undergone by women and machines have destabilized the supremacy of men but not yet destroyed it.

As *Mann and Machine* illustrates, the boundaries separating men, women, and machines are in a state of flux during the late twentieth

century. Conventional ways of defining what makes each one unique have
started to give way, and the human body has become a terrain of dispute.
Ambivalence about the human body has manifested itself in various ways
in the past, but at no other time has serious speculation about bodily
obsolescence been joined by a glut of mass-media imagery depicting a
posthuman future. Nevertheless, despite the prevalence of posthuman
imagery, a desire to preserve bodily pleasures clearly remains. There is,
however, no consensus on how posthuman pleasures should be experienced. Perhaps, as J. G. Ballard warns in *Crash*, the cybernetic fusion of
human beings with technology is leading to an era when pleasure and
pain will become indistinguishable. Alternatively, perhaps we can still
anticipate the pleasure of a new beginning, one in which technology will
become part of an egalitarian social configuration and inequalities will
be rejected as anachronisms from a bygone age that was merely human.

NOTES

INTRODUCTION: TECHNO-EROTICISM

1. K. C. D'Alessandro, "Technophilia: Cyberpunk and Cinema," paper delivered at the Society for Cinema Studies Conference, Bozeman, Montana, July 1988, 1.

2. Fredric Jameson, "Postmodernism, or the Cultural Logic of Late Capitalism," *New Left Review* 146 (July–August 1984): 79.

3. J. G. Ballard, *Crash* (New York: Vintage, 1985 [1973]).

4. Ibid., 112.

5. Ibid., 16.

6. J. G. Ballard, interview by Graeme Revell, *Re/Search* 8/9 (1984): 49.

7. J. G. Ballard, "Introduction to the French Edition" (French ed., Paris: Calmann-Levy, 1974). Introduction appears in the original English in *Foundation* 9 (November 1975); reprinted in Ballard, *Crash*, 6.

8. Jean Baudrillard, "Ballard's *Crash,*" *Science-Fiction Studies* 18, no. 55, part 3 (November 1991): 313–320.

9. N. Katherine Hayles, "In Response to Jean Baudrillard: The Borders of Madness," *Science-Fiction Studies* 18, no. 55, part 3 (November 1991): 321–23; 323.

10. Vivian Sobchack, "Baudrillard's Obscenity," *Science-Fiction Studies* 18, no. 55, part 3 (November 1991): 327–329; 328, 329.

11. Vivian Sobchack, "New Age Mutant Ninja Hackers: Reading *Mondo 2000,*" *South Atlantic Quarterly* 92, no. 4 (fall 1993): 569–584.

12. Ballard, *Crash,* 179.

13. John Tierney, "Porn, the Low-Slung Engine of Progress," *New York Times,* 9 January 1994, section 2. The following quotations from Tierney are all from this article.

14. Jim Starlin and Diana Graziunas, *Lady El* (New York: ROC, 1992).

15. Chris Weedon, *Feminist Practice and Poststructuralist Theory* (Oxford: Blackwell, 1987), 2.

16. Ibid.

CHAPTER 1: DELETING THE BODY

1. Jean-François Lyotard, "Can Thought Go on without a Body?" trans. Bruce Boone and Lee Hildreth, *Discourse* 11, no. 1 (1988–1989): 74–87.

2. René Descartes, *Discourse on Method and Meditations,* trans. Laurence J. Lafleur (Indianapolis: Bobbs-Merrill, 1960), 42.

3. Steven Levy, *Artificial Life: The Quest for a New Creation* (New York: Pantheon, 1992), 9.

4. Mary Jacobus, Evelyn Fox Keller, and Sally Shuttleworth, eds., *Body/Politics: Women and the Discourses of Science* (New York: Routledge, 1990), 5.

5. Sherry Turkle, *The Second Self: Computers and the Human Spirit* (New York: Simon and Schuster, 1984).

6. J. David Bolter, *Turing's Man: Western Culture in the Computer Age* (Chapel Hill: University of North Carolina Press, 1984).

7. David Tomas, "Old Rituals for New Space: *Rites de Passage* and William Gibson's Cultural Model of Cyberspace," in *Cyberspace: First Steps,* ed. Michael Benedikt, 31–47 (Cambridge: MIT Press, 1991), 32.

8. Levy, *Artificial Life,* 5.

9. Maureen Caudill, *In Our Own Image: Building an Artificial Person* (Oxford: Oxford University Press, 1992), 14.

10. David H. Freedman, "If He Only Had a Brain," *Discover* 13, no. 8 (August 1992): 54–60.

11. Pamela McCorduck, *Machines Who Think* (San Francisco: W. H. Freeman, 1979), 357.

12. Moravec quoted in Grant Fjermedal, *The Tomorrow Makers: A Brave New World of Living-Brain Machines* (New York: Macmillan, 1986), 8.

13. Hans Moravec, *Mind Children: The Future of Robot and Human Intelligence* (Cambridge, Mass.: Harvard University Press, 1988), 1.

14. Fjermedal, *Tomorrow Makers*, 249.

15. Roger Penrose, *The Emperor's New Mind* (Oxford: Oxford University Press, 1989); Penrose, *Shadows of the Mind: A Search for the Missing Science of Consciousness* (Oxford: Oxford University Press, 1994). The quotations are from *The Emperor's New Mind*, 447.

16. Ibid., 407.

17. Michael Blumlein, in "Is the Body Obsolete? A Forum," *Whole Earth Review* 63 (1989): 34–55; quotation on 55.

18. Starhawk, in ibid., 35.

19. The following opinions, from Kathy Acker's through Mark Pauline's, are all from ibid. Page numbers are given parenthetically in the text.

20. Bolter, *Turing's Man*, 201.

21. McCorduck, *Machines Who Think*, 14.

22. Neil Frude, *The Intimate Machine: Close Encounters with Computers and Robots* (New York: New American Library, 1983), 148–149.

23. "Vision Research Tests Idea of Computer Chip for Sight," *Providence Sunday Journal*, 5 July 1992.

24. Moravec, *Mind Children*, 116–117.

25. Minsky, in "Is the Body Obsolete?" 37.

26. Marvin Minsky, *The Society of Mind* (New York: Simon and Schuster, 1985), 328.

27. Constance Penley, *The Future of an Illusion* (Minneapolis: University of Minnesota Press, 1989), 121.

28. Ian Edginton and Vince Giarrano, *The Terminator* 1–4 (Milwaukie, Ore.: Dark Horse Comics, 1991–1992).

29. Frank Miller and Walter Simonson, *RoboCop versus the Terminator* 1–4 (Milwaukie, Ore.: Dark Horse Comics, 1992).

30. Scott Bukatman, *Terminal Identity: The Virtual Subject in Postmodern Science Fiction* (Durham, N.C.: Duke University Press, 1993); Larry McCaffery, ed., *Storming the Reality Studio: A Casebook of Cyberpunk and Postmodern Fiction* (Durham, N.C.: Duke University Press, 1991); George Slusser and Tom Shippey, eds., *Fiction 2000: Cyberpunk and the Future of Narrative* (Athens: University of Georgia Press, 1992).

31. William Gibson, *Neuromancer* (New York: Ace, 1984); Gibson, *Count Zero* (New York: Ace, 1986); Gibson, *Mona Lisa Overdrive* (New York: Bantam, 1988).

32. Rudy Rucker, *Software* (New York: Avon Books, 1982).

33. Hans Moravec, interview by David Turin, *Mondo 2000* 11 (1993): 47–51; 51.

34. J. G. Ballard, "Introduction to the French Edition" (French ed., Paris: Calmann-Levy, 1974). Introduction appears in the original English in *Foundation* 9 (November 1975); reprinted in Ballard, *Crash* (New York: Vintage, 1985), 4–5.

35. Donna Haraway, "Manifesto for Cyborgs: Science, Technology, and Socialist Feminism in the 1980s," *Socialist Review* 80 (1985): 65–107. Reprinted in Haraway, *Simians, Cyborgs, and Women: The Reinvention of Nature* (New York: Routledge, 1991), 149–181.

36. Fredric Jameson, *Postmodernism, or, The Cultural Logic of Late Capitalism* (Durham, N.C.: Duke University Press, 1991), 419.

37. George Alec Effinger, *When Gravity Fails* (New York: Bantam, 1987); Effinger, *A Fire in the Sun* (New York: Bantam, 1990); Effinger, *The Exile Kiss* (New York: Bantam, 1991).

38. Effinger, *Fire in the Sun*, 234.

39. Jean Baudrillard, *Simulations*, trans. Paul Foss, Paul Patton, and Philip Beitchman (New York: Semiotext(e), 1983), 4.

40. James Tiptree Jr., *The Girl Who Was Plugged In* (New York: TOR, 1973).

41. "New Wrinkle in Cosmetics Poses Ugly Questions," *Providence Sunday Journal*, 4 August 1991.

42. Gibson, *Count Zero*, 101.

43. Walter Jon Williams, *Hardwired* (New York: TOR, 1986), 25.

44. Effinger, *When Gravity Fails*, 14.

45. Bruce Sterling, *Schismatrix* (New York: Ace Science Fiction, 1985); Sterling, *Crystal Express* (New York: Ace, 1990).

46. Bruce Sterling, "Twenty Evocations," *Crystal Express*, 107.

47. Bolter, *Turing's Man*, xii.

48. Ibid., 8.

49. Descartes, *Discourse*, 138.

50. Ibid., 41–42.

51. Aram Vartanian, *La Mettrie's L'Homme Machine: A Study in the Origins of an Idea* (Princeton, N.J.: Princeton University Press, 1960), cited in Bolter, *Turing's Man*, 205.

52. Minsky quoted in McCorduck, *Machines Who Think*, 70.

53. Jameson, *Postmodernism*.

54. Arthur and Marilouise Kroker, eds., *Body Invaders: Panic Sex in America* (New York: St. Martin's, 1987), 22.

55. William Gibson, *Virtual Light* (New York: Bantam, 1993), 264.

56. Jameson, *Postmodernism*, 39–45.

57. William Gibson, interview, in *Cyberpunk* (video; Intercon Productions, 1990).

58. Gibson, *Neuromancer*, 12.

59. Effinger, *Fire in the Sun*, 26.

60. Gibson, *Virtual Light*, 134.

61. Effinger, *Fire in the Sun*, 284.

62. Jean Baudrillard, *Xerox and Infinity*, trans. Agitac (Paris: Touchepas, 1988), 7.

63. Scott Bukatman, *Terminal Identity*.

64. Vivian Sobchack, *Screening Space* (New York: Ungar, 1991), 257.

65. Ibid., 231–232.

66. Tom Forester, *High-Tech Society: The Story of the Information Technology Revolution* (Cambridge, Mass.: MIT Press, 1987), 18.

67. Ibid., 1.

68. Jean-François Lyotard, *The Postmodern Condition: A Report on Knowledge*, trans. Geoff Bennington and Brian Massumi (Minneapolis: University of Minnesota Press, 1984), 67.

69. Manuel De Landa, *War in the Age of Intelligent Machines* (New York: Zone, 1991), 128.

70. Ibid., 230.

71. Lyotard, *Postmodern Condition*, 37, 29, 66.

72. N. Katherine Hayles, "Text out of Context: Situating Postmodernism within an Information Society," *Discourse* 9 (spring-summer 1987): 33–34.

73. Sandra Harding, *Whose Science? Whose Knowledge?* (Ithaca, N.Y.: Cornell University Press, 1991), 37.

74. Ibid., 37, 44.

75. Donna Haraway, *Primate Visions: Gender, Race, and Nature in the World of Modern Science* (New York: Routledge, 1989).

76. Joan Rothschild, ed., *Machina Ex Dea: Feminist Perspectives on Technology* (New York: Pergamon, 1983).

77. Joan Rothschild, *Teaching Technology from a Feminist Perspective* (New York: Pergamon, 1988).

78. Haraway, *Primate Visions*; Avital Ronell, interview by Andrea Juno, in *Angry Women*, ed. Andrea Juno and V. Vale (San Francisco: Re/Search, 1991), 127–153; Valie Export, "The Real and Its Double: The Body," *Discourse* 11 (fall-winter, 1988–1989): 3–27.

CHAPTER 2: THE PLEASURE OF THE INTERFACE

1. J. G. Ballard, interview by Peter Linnett, *Corridor* 5 (1974); reprinted in *Re/Search* 8–9 (1984): 164.

2. J. G. Ballard, interview by Lynn Barber, *Penthouse*, September 1970; reprinted in *Re/Search* 8–9:157.

3. Lee Hart is quoted in Dale Riepe, "Review of *Philosophy and Cybernetics*, ed. Crosson and Sayre," *Technology and Culture* 9 (October 1968): 627; see also Joan Rothschild, "Introduction," in *Machina Ex Dea: Feminist Perspectives on Technology*, ed. Joan Rothschild, ix–xxix (New York: Pergamon, 1983), xix.

4. Jack B. Rochester and John Gantz, *The Naked Computer: A Layperson's Almanac of Computer Lore, Wizardry, Personalities, Memorabilia, World Records, Mind Blowers and Tomfoolery* (New York: William and Morrow, 1983), 11.

5. "Micro Chic: Artificial Intelligence to Wear," *Mondo 2000* 1 (1989): 80–83.

6. Queen Mu, "Bacchic Pleasures," *Mondo 2000* 5 (n.d.): 80–81.

7. Chris Hudak, "Head from a Binaural Dummy: 3D-CD 'Virtual Reality' Erotica," *Mondo 2000* 11 (1993): 123–124.

8. Phillip Robinson and Nancy Tamosaitis, *The Joy of Cybersex: An Underground Guide to Electronic Erotica* (New York: Brady, 1993).

9. "*BodyCello* Adult Computer Software Catalog" (Sorrento Valley, Calif.: BodyCello), 7.

10. "Nightwatch Interactive CD-ROM," BodyCello Adults Only Software, BodyCello, Sorrento Valley, Calif.

11. Rochester and Gantz, *Naked Computer*, 85–86.

12. Mike Saenz, interview by Jeff Milstead and Jude Milhon, *Mondo 2000* 4 (n.d.): 142–144.

13. Ibid., 143.

14. "For Some, Computer Sex Pushes the Right Buttons," *Providence Sunday Journal*, 8 March 1992.

15. Suzanne Stefanac, "Sex and the New Media," *NewMedia* 3, no. 4 (April 1993): 38–45; 39.

16. Mark Dery, "Sex Machine, Machine Sex: Mechano-Eroticism and Robo-Copulation," *Mondo 2000* 5 (n.d.): 42–43.

17. Walter Kendrick, *The Secret Museum: Pornography in Modern Culture* (New York: Penguin, 1987), 31.

18. Donna Haraway, "Manifesto for Cyborgs: Science, Technology, and Socialist Feminism in the 1980s," *Socialist Review* 80 (1985): 65–107; reprinted in Haraway, *Simians, Cyborgs, and Women: The Reinvention of Nature* (New York: Routledge, 1991), 149-181; quotation on 152.

19. Andreas Huyssen, "The Vamp and the Machine: Technology and Sexuality in Fritz Lang's *Metropolis*," *New German Critique* 24–25 (1981–1982): 221–237.

20. K. C. D'Alessandro, "Technophilia: Cyberpunk and Cinema," paper delivered at the Society for Cinema Studies conference, Bozeman, Montana, July 1988, 1.

21. William Gibson, *Virtual Light* (New York: Bantam, 1993), 251.

22. Scott Bukatman, *Virtual Identity: The Virtual Subject in Postmodern Science Fiction* (Durham, N.C.: Duke University Press, 1993), 244.

23. Sigmund Freud, "The 'Uncanny'" (1919), in *The Standard Edition of the Complete Psychological Works of Sigmund Freud*, ed. and trans. James Strachey, 24 vols. (London: Hogarth, 1973), 17:219–252.

24. Denis de Rougemont, *Love in the Western World* (New York: Harper and Row, 1956), 243.

25. Rudolph Binion, *Love beyond Death: The Anatomy of a Myth in the Arts* (New York: New York University Press, 1993), 3, 9, 97.

26. Scott Rockwell and Darryl Banks, *Cyberpunk* 1: vol. 1, no. 1 .

27. George Alec Effinger, *When Gravity Fails* (New York: Bantam, 1987); Effinger, *A Fire in the Sun* (New York: Bantam, 1990); Effinger, *The Exile Kiss* (New York: Bantam, 1991).

28. Walter Jon Williams, *Hardwired* (New York: TOR, 1986), 25.

29. Donna Haraway, "A Manifesto for Cyborgs"; reprinted in Haraway, *Simians, Cyborgs, and Women*, 149–181.

30. Constance Penley and Andrew Ross, "Cyborgs at Large: Interview with Donna Haraway," in *Technoculture*, ed. Constance Penley and Andrew Ross, 1–20 (Minneapolis: University of Minnesota Press, 1991).

31. Janet Bergstrom, "Androids and Androgyny," *Camera Obscura* 15 (1986): 39.

32. Hans Moravec, interview, *Omni* 11, no. 11 (1989): 88.

33. Lyotard, "Can Thought Go on without a Body?" 86.

34. Jean Baudrillard, *Xerox and Infinity*, trans. Agitac (Paris: Touchepas, 1988), 3.

35. Ibid., 16.

36. James D. Hudnall and Paul Johnson, *Interface* 1, no. 1 (New York: Epic Comics, 1989).

37. Gibson, *Virtual Light*, 272.

38. Baudrillard, *Xerox and Infinity*, 5–6.

39. William Gibson, "High Tech/High Life" (interview by Timothy Leary), *Mondo 2000* 1 (1989): 61.

40. William Gibson, *Neuromancer* (New York: Ace, 1984); Gibson, *Count Zero* (New York: Ace, 1986); Gibson, *Mona Lisa Overdrive* (New York: Bantam, 1988).

41. Gibson, *Neuromancer*, 51.

42. Nicola Nixon, "Cyberpunk: Preparing the Ground for Revolution or Keeping

the Boys Satisfied?" *Science-Fiction Studies* 57 (July 1992): 219–235; quotation on 226.

43. Ibid., 227.

44. Gibson, *Neuromancer*, 5.

45. Ibid., 6.

46. Ibid., 256.

47. Williams, *Hardwired*, 51.

48. Ibid., 50.

49. Andrew Ross, *Strange Weather: Culture, Science, and Technology in the Age of Limits* (London: Verso, 1991), 152–153.

50. Williams, *Hardwired*, 340.

51. Ibid., 5.

52. Loyd Blankenship, *GURPS Cyberpunk High-Tech Low-Life Roleplaying Sourcebook* (Austin, Tx.: Steve Jackson Games, 1990), 72.

53. Rockwell and Banks, *Cyberpunk* 2: vol. 1, no. 2 (Wheeling, W. Va.: Innovative Corporation, 1990).

54. Michel Foucault, *The Order of Things: An Archaeology of the Human Sciences* (New York: Vintage Books, 1973), 387.

CHAPTER 3: VIRTUAL SEX

1. Michael Saenz, "The Carpal Tunnel of Love: Virtual Sex with Mike Saenz" (interview by Jeff Milstead and Jude Milhon), *Mondo 2000* 4 (n.d.): 143.

2. Linda Williams, "Film Body: An Implantation of Perversions," *Cine-Tracts* 12 (winter 1981); reprinted in *Narrative, Apparatus, Ideology: A Film Theory Reader*, ed. Phillip Rosen, 507–534 (New York: Columbia University Press, 1986); Williams, *Hard Core: Power, Pleasure, and the "Frenzy of the Visible"* (Berkeley: University of California Press, 1989).

3. John Perry Barlow, "Being in Nothingness," *Mondo 2000* 2 (summer 1990): 34–43.

4. Chet Raymo, "Flights of Cyber-fancy," *Boston Globe*, 23 March 1992.

5. Allucquere Rosanne Stone, "Will the Real Body Please Stand Up?: Boundary Stories about Virtual Cultures," in *Cyberspace: First Steps*, ed. Michael Benedikt, 81–118 (Cambridge, Mass.: MIT Press, 1991), 105.

6. Barlow, "Being," 42.

7. Saenz, "Carpal Tunnel," 143–144.

8. Howard Rheingold, "Teledildonics: Reach out and Touch Someone," *Mondo 2000* 2 (summer 1990): 52–54; 54.

9. Howard Rheingold, *Virtual Reality* (New York: Summit, 1991), 348.

10. Rheingold, *Virtual Reality*, 349.

11. Mark Dery, "Guerilla Semiotics: Sex Machine, Machine Sex: Mechano-Eroticism & RoboCopulation," *Mondo 2000* 5 (n.d.): 43.

12. The following quotations from Michael Heim are from his essay "The Erotic Ontology of Cyberspace," in *Cyberspace: First Steps*, ed. Michael Benedikt, 59–80 (Cambridge, Mass.: MIT Press, 1991). Page numbers are given parenthetically in text.

13. Fredric Jameson, *Postmodernism, or, The Cultural Logic of Late Capitalism* (Durham, N.C.: Duke University Press, 1991), 38–45.

14. The following quotations from Nicole Stenger are from her essay "Mind Is a

Leaking Rainbow," in *Cyberspace: First Steps*, ed. Michael Benedikt, 49–58 (Cambridge, Mass.: MIT Press, 1991). Page numbers are given parenthetically in text.

15. Donna Haraway, "A Manifesto for Cyborgs: Science, Technology, and Socialist Feminism in the 1980s," *Socialist Review* 80 (1985): 65–107; reprinted in Haraway, *Simians, Cyborgs, and Women: The Reinvention of Nature* (New York: Routledge, 1991), 149–181.

16. Klaus Theweleit, *Male Fantasies*, 2 vols. (vol. 1, *Women, Floods, Bodies, History*, trans. Stephen Conway [Minneapolis: University of Minnesota Press, 1987]; vol. 2, *Psychoanalyzing the White Terror*, trans. Erica Carter and Chris Turner [Minneapolis: University of Minnesota Press, 1989]).

17. Brenda Laurel, quoted in Suzanne Stefanac, "Sex and the New Media," *NewMedia* 3, no. 4 (April 1993): 38–45; 41.

18. Mike Saenz, quoted in ibid., 41.

19. Ibid.

20. Mike Saenz, quoted in Johnny Dodd, "Virtual Sex: A Peek at the High-Tech Sexual Future," *Providence Phoenix*, 18 March 1993, 5.

21. Jude Milhon, quoted in ibid., 5.

22. Linda Jacobson, quoted in Stefanac, "Sex," 41.

23. Susie Bright, *Sexual Reality: A Virtual Sex World Reader* (Pittsburgh, Pa.: Cleis, 1992), 65.

24. Vivian Sobchack, "New Age Mutant Ninja Hackers," *Artforum International* 29, no. 8 (April 1991): 24–25.

25. Ibid., 25.

26. Scott Bukatman, *Terminal Identity: The Virtual Subject in Postmodern Science Fiction* (Durham, N.C.: Duke University Press, 1993), 190.

27. Jeff Milstead and Jude Milhon, "Introduction to 'The Carpal Tunnel of Love: Virtual Sex with Mike Saenz,'" *Mondo 2000* 4 (n.d.): 142.

28. Stone, "Will the Real Body," 109.

CHAPTER 4: MUSCULAR CIRCUITRY

1. Kathy Acker, *Empire of the Senseless* (New York: Grove, 1988), 210.

2. Hans Moravec, *Mind Children: The Future of Robot and Human Intelligence* (Cambridge, Mass.: Harvard University Press, 1988).

3. Janet Bergstrom, "Androids and Androgyny," in *Close Encounters: Film Feminism, and Science Fiction*, ed. Constance Penley, et al., 33–60 (Minneapolis: University of Minnesota Press, 1991).

4. Constance Penley, *The Future of an Illusion* (Minneapolis: University of Minnesota Press, 1989), 132.

5. Lynne Joyrich, "Television and the Cyborg Subject(ed)," University of Wisconsin Center for Twentieth Century Studies Working Paper no. 8 (Milwaukee: University of Wisconsin Center for Twentieth Century Studies, 1989–1990), 15.

6. Steven Neale, "Masculinity as Spectacle: Reflections on Men and Mainstream Cinema," *Screen* 24, no. 6 (1983): 37.

7. Roger Hahn, "The Meaning of the Mechanistic Age," in *The Boundaries of Humanity: Humans, Animals, Machines*, ed. James J. Sheehan and Morton Sosna, 142–157 (Berkeley: University of California Press, 1991), 145.

8. Ibid., 146.

9. Ibid., 147.

10. Karel Čapek, *R.U.R.* (London: Oxford University Press, 1964 [1920]).

11. Isaac Asimov and Karen A. Frenkel, *Robots: Machines in Man's Image* (New York: Harmony, 1985), 12.

12. Jean Baudrillard, *Simulations*, trans. Paul Foss, Paul Patton, and Philip Beitchman (New York: Semiotext(e), 1983), 92–93.

13. Ibid., 93–94.

14. Bruce Sterling, "CATscan: Cyber-Superstition," *Science Fiction Eye* 8 (winter 1991): 11–12; 11.

15. Mary Ann Doane, "Technophilia: Technology, Representation, and the Feminine," in *Body/Politics: Women and the Discourses of Science*, ed. Mary Jacobus, Evelyn Fox Keller, and Sally Shuttleworth, 163–176 (New York: Routledge, 1990), 163.

16. Thomas Laqueur, *Making Sex: Body and Gender from the Greeks to Freud* (Cambridge, Mass.: Harvard University Press, 1990).

17. Ibid., 126–127.

18. Ibid., 35–43.

19. J. David Bolter, *Turing's Man: Western Culture in the Computer Age* (Chapel Hill: University of North Carolina Press, 1984), 8.

20. Andrew Ross, *Strange Weather: Culture, Science and Technology in the Age of Limits* (New York: Verso, 1991), 137–167.

21. Nicola Nixon, "Cyberpunk: Preparing the Ground for Revolution or Keeping the Boys Satisfied?" *Science-Fiction Studies* 57 (July 1992): 219–235.

22. Donna Haraway, "A Manifesto for Cyborgs: Science, Technology, and Socialist Feminism in the 1980s," *Socialist Review* 80 (1985): 65–107; reprinted in Haraway, *Simians, Cyborgs, and Women: The Reinvention of Nature* (New York: Routledge, 1991), 149–181.

23. Avital Ronell, interview by Andrea Juno, in *Angry Women*, ed. Andrea Juno and V. Vale, 127–153 (San Francisco: Re/Search, 1991).

24. Valie Export, "The Real and Its Double: The Body," *Discourse* 11, no. 1 (fall/winter 1988–1989): 3–27.

25. Haraway, "Manifesto," 70.

26. Penley, "Time Travel," 124.

27. Vivian Sobchack, "Child/Alien/Father: Patriarchal Crisis and Generic Exchange," in *Close Encounters: Film, Feminism, and Science Fiction*, ed. Constance Penley, et al., 3–30 (Minneapolis: University of Minnesota Press, 1991), 23.

28. Klaus Theweleit, *Male Fantasies*, 2 vols. (vol. 1, *Women, Floods, Bodies, History*, trans. Stephen Conway [Minneapolis: University of Minnesota Press, 1987]; vol. 2, *Psychoanalyzing the White Terror*, trans. Erica Carter and Chris Turner [Minneapolis: University of Minnesota Press, 1989]).

29. Hal Foster, "Armor Fou," *October* 56 (spring 1991): 65–97.

30. Mark Dery, "Cyborging the Body Politic," *Mondo 2000* 6 (1992): 103.

31. Ibid., 102.

32. The treatment of technology and women in the film *Metropolis* is analyzed in Andreas Huyssen, "The Vamp and the Machine: Technology and Sexuality in Fritz Lang's *Metropolis*," *New German Critique* 24–25 (1981–1982): 221–237; Doane, "Technophilia," 163–176; and Roger Dadoun, "*Metropolis*: Mother-City—'Mittler'—

Hitler," in *Close Encounters: Film, Feminism, and Science Fiction*, ed. Constance Penley, et al., 133–159 (Minneapolis: University of Minnesota Press, 1991).

33. Cynthia J. Fuchs, "'Death Is Irrelevant': Cyborgs, Reproduction, and the Future of Male Hysteria," *Genders* 18 (Winter 1993): 126.

34. Vivian Sobchack, "The Virginity of Astronauts," in *Shadows of the Magic Lamp: Fantasy and Science Fiction in Film*, ed. George Slusser and Eric S. Rabkin, 41–57 (Carbondale: Southern Illinois University Press, 1985), 47, 48.

35. Frank Miller and Geof Darrow, *Hard Boiled* 1 (Milwaukie, Ore.: Dark Horse Comics, September 1990).

36. Miller and Darrow, *Hard Boiled* 2 (Milwaukie, Ore.: Dark Horse Comics, December 1990).

37. Miller and Darrow, *Hard Boiled* 3 (Milwaukie, Ore.: Dark Horse Comics, March 1992).

38. Fredric Jameson, "Postmodernism, or the Cultural Logic of Late Capitalism," *New Left Review* 146 (July-August 1984): 53–92; reprinted in Fredric Jameson, *Postmodernism, or, The Cultural Logic of Late Capitalism* (Durham, N.C.: Duke University Press, 1991), 1–54.

CHAPTER 5: DIGITAL RAGE

1. Walter Jon Williams, *Hardwired* (New York: TOR, 1986), 16.

2. Sherry Turkle, *The Second Self: Computers and the Human Spirit* (New York: Simon and Schuster, 1984), 313.

3. A recent text that describes the imagined thoughts of a robotic historian is Manuel De Landa's *War in the Age of Intelligent Machines* (New York: Zone, 1991).

4. See Turkle, *Second Self*, for an analysis of how young people tend to anthropomorphize computers and also to think of themselves as machines.

5. Jack B. Rochester and John Gantz, *The Naked Computer: A Layperson's Almanac of Computer Lore, Wizardry, Personalities, Memorabilia, World Records, Mind Blowers and Tomfoolery* (New York: William Morrow, 1983), 66.

6. Four of the many texts that draw close analogies between human memory and computer memory are Roger C. Schank and Kenneth Mark Colby, eds., *Computer Models of Thought and Language* (San Francisco: W.H. Freeman: 1973); Peter H. Lindsay and Donald A. Norman, *Human Information Processing: An Introduction to Psychology* (New York: Academic, 1977); Roger C. Schank, *Explanation Patterns: Understanding Mechanically and Creatively* (Hillsdale, N.J.: Erlbaum, 1986); and Wayne Wickelgren, *Cognitive Psychology* (Englewood Cliffs, N.J.: Prentice-Hall, 1979). An opposing point of view is provided by Roger Penrose in *The Emperor's New Mind* (Oxford: Oxford University Press, 1989).

7. J. David Bolter, *Turing's Man: Western Culture in the Computer Age* (Chapel Hill: University of North Carolina Press, 1984), 198.

8. Turkle, *Second Self*, 309.

9. Bolter, *Turing's Man*, 221.

10. Schank, *Explanation Patterns*, 230.

11. Frank Rich, "Fear of AIDS Injects the New Blood Culture into the National Mainstream," *Providence Sunday Journal*, 13 December 1992.

12. Donna Haraway, "A Manifesto for Cyborgs: Science, Technology, and Socialist

Feminism in the 1980s," *Socialist Review* 80 (1985): 65–107; reprinted in Haraway, *Simians, Cyborgs, and Women: The Reinvention of Nature* (New York: Routledge, 1991), 149–181.

13. Marvin Minsky, *The Society of Mind* (New York: Simon and Schuster, 1986), 289.

14. See Jean-François Lyotard, *The Postmodern Condition: A Report on Knowledge*, trans. Geoff Bennington and Brian Massumi (Minneapolis: University of Minnesota Press, 1984).

15. Jean Baudrillard, *Simulations*, trans. Paul Foss, Paul Patton, and Philip Beitchman (New York: Semiotext(e), 1983).

16. Hans Moravec, *Mind Children: The Future of Robot and Human Intelligence* (Cambridge, Mass.: Harvard University Press, 1988), 108.

17. George Alec Effinger, *When Gravity Fails* (New York: Bantam, 1987); Effinger, *A Fire in the Sun* (New York: Bantam, 1990); Effinger, *The Exile Kiss* (New York: Bantam, 1991).

18. Effinger, *When Gravity Fails*, 240–243, 257, 286.

19. William Gibson, *Neuromancer* (New York: Ace, 1984); Gibson, *Count Zero* (New York: Ace, 1986); Gibson, *Mona Lisa Overdrive* (New York: Bantam, 1988).

20. Effinger, *When Gravity Fails*, 42.

21. Ibid., 171.

22. Effinger, *Fire in the Sun*, 86.

23. Gabriele Schwab, "Cyborgs: Postmodern Phantasms of Body and Mind," *Discourse* 9 (spring-summer 1987): 81.

24. John Varley, "Overdrawn at the Memory Bank," in *The Persistence of Vision*, 197–226 (New York: Dial, 1978), 216.

25. Ibid., 210–211.

26. Pat Cadigan, *Mindplayers* (New York: Bantam, 1987).

27. Williams, *Hardwired*, 293.

28. Ibid., 226.

29. Marv Wolfman and George Perez, *Tales of the New Teen Titans* 1 (New York: DC Comics, June 1982).

30. Timothy Leary, "Quark of the Decade?" *Mondo 2000* 1 (1989): 53–56; 56.

31. Nicola Nixon, "Cyberpunk: Preparing the Ground for Revolution or Keeping the Boys Satisfied?" *Science-Fiction Studies* 57 (July 1992): 219–235; quotation on 222.

32. John J. Pierce, "On Three Matters in SFS #57," *Science-Fiction Studies* 58 (November 1992): 440.

33. William Gibson, "Johnny Mnemonic," in *Burning Chrome*, 1–22 (New York: Ace, 1986).

34. Gibson, *Neuromancer*, 25, 24, 25, 147.

35. Andrew Ross, *Strange Weather: Culture, Science, and Technology in the Age of Limits* (London: Verso, 1991), 158.

36. Frank Miller and Bill Sienkiewicz, *Elektra Assassin* 1–8 (New York: Epic Comics, 1986–1987).

37. Kathy Acker, *Empire of the Senseless* (New York: Grove, 1988).

38. Williams, *Hardwired*, 16.

39. Chris Todd and Doug Talalla, *Seraphim* 1, no. 1 (Wheeling, W.Va.: Innovative Corporation, May 1990).

40. Frank Miller and Walter Simonson, *RoboCop versus the Terminator* 1–4 (Milwaukie, Ore.: Dark Horse Comics, 1992).

41. Mark Dery, "Cyborging the Body Politic," *Mondo 2000* 6 (1992): 103.

42. Scott Bukatman cites Bruce Sterling's Shaper/Mechanist series as a somewhat unique example of a radically posthuman future in "Postcards from the Posthuman Solar System," *Science-Fiction Studies* 55 (November 1991): 343–357.

43. Jean-François Lyotard, "Can Thought Go on without a Body?" trans. Bruce Boone and Lee Hildreth, *Discourse* 11 no. 1 (fall-winter 1988–89): 74–87; quotations on 85, 86.

44. The following quotations from the novel are from Jim Starlin and Diana Graziunas, *Lady El* (New York: ROC, 1992). Page numbers are given parenthetically in the text.

45. Schwab's discussion in "Cyborgs" of the "holonomy of the subject," in which the complete information of a person is stored in each of his or her parts, is relevant here.

46. Brooks Landon, "Bet on It: Cyber Video Punk Performance," *Mondo 2000* 1 (1989): 142–145.

CHAPTER 6: MEN AND MACHINE-WOMEN

1. Villiers de l'Isle-Adam, *L'Eve future* (1886; published in English as *Tomorrow's Eve*, trans. Robert Martin Adams [Urbana: University of Illinois Press, 1982]).

2. Annette Michelson, "On the Eve of the Future: The Reasonable Facsimile and the Philosophical Toy," in *October: The First Decade, 1976–1986*, ed. Annette Michelson, et al., 416–435 (Cambridge, Mass.: MIT Press, 1987).

3. The following quotations are from Hajime Sorayama, *Sexy Robot* (Tokyo: Genko-sha, 1983).

4. Andreas Huyssen, "The Vamp and the Machine: Technology and Sexuality in Fritz Lang's *Metropolis*," *New German Critique* 24–25 (1981–82): 221–237.

5. Ibid., 235.

6. Fredric Jameson, "Postmodernism, or the Cultural Logic of Late Capitalism," *New Left Review* 146 (July-August 1984): 53–92; reprinted in Fredric Jameson, *Postmodernism, or, The Cultural Logic of Late Capitalism*, 1–54 (Durham, N.C.: Duke University Press, 1991).

7. Roger Dadoun, "*Metropolis*: Mother-City—'Mittler'—Hitler," in *Close Encounters: Film, Feminism, and Science Fiction*, ed. Constance Penley, et al., 133–159 (Minneapolis: University of Minnesota Press, 1991).

8. Jameson, "Postmodernism," 79.

9. Donna Haraway, "A Manifesto for Cyborgs: Science, Technology and Socialist Feminism in the 1980s," *Socialist Review* 80 (1985): 65–107; reprinted in Haraway, *Simians, Cyborgs, and Women: The Reinvention of Nature*, 149–181 (New York: Routledge, 1991). This quotation is from page 70 in the first publication.

10. Ibid.

11. Jean Baudrillard, *Simulations*, trans. Paul Foss, Paul Patton, and Philip Beitchman (New York: Semiotext(e), 1983).

INDEX

Acker, Kathy, 24, 136–137
"After Dark," 54
AI. *See* Artificial intelligence (AI)
AIDS, 10, 71, 84, 128
Aizawa, Masuo, 21
Amnesia, historical, 40
Androgyny, 97
Androids, compared with cyborgs, 20
"Androids and Androgyny" (Bergstrom), 97
Annihilators, The, 30
Artificial intelligence (AI), 20–21, 23, 26, 30, 67, 126–127, 130, 140
Artificial life, 16–17, 21, 28–29

Artificial Life (Levy), 21
Automata, 28–29, 57, 100, 101
Automobiles, techno-eroticism of, 4, 5–8

Bacon, Francis, 100
Ballard, J.G., 5–8, 12, 33, 50, 51, 161
Barlow, John Perry, 81–82
Baudrillard, Jean, 6–7, 34, 43, 67–68, 71–72, 88, 101, 130, 158
Bellmer, Hans, 109
Bergstrom, Janet, 67, 97
Binion, Rudolph, 62
Blade Runner, 20, 132–133, 147, 153
Blumlein, Michael, 23, 24

Boardwatch, 55
Bodiless sexuality, 61–64, 68–70, 83–84.
    See also Sexuality; Virtual reality
Body: ambivalence toward, 55–56;
    bodiless sexuality, 61–64, 83–84; as
    "meat" in cyberpunk, 62, 64; mind/
    body duality, 23, 31–32, 34, 49;
    obsolescence of, in cyberpunk
    science fiction, 31–38; panic bodies in
    postmodernist consumer society, 40;
    responses to bodily obsolescence,
    23–27; vulnerability of, in late
    twentieth century, 71, 84, 128; women
    associated with, 49. *See also* Sexuality
Bolter, J. David, 18, 28, 38, 39, 104, 127
Brain: compared with computers, 13,
    124–130; downloading human
    consciousness into brain machine,
    26, 129–130; as "meat" machine, 39
Brain machine, 26, 129–130
Brainstorm, 83
Bram Stoker's Dracula, 128
Bright, Susie, 53, 90
Bukatman, Scott, 31, 43–44, 58, 91
Bulletin boards about sex, 55
Burroughs, William, 26–27
Butler, Octavia, 67

Capek, Karel, 101
Cadigan, Pat, 134
Carnegie Mellon University, 22
Caudill, Maureen, 21
CD–ROMS, sex software on, 53–54, 80
Cherry 2000, 29, 148
Clock metaphor, 38–39
Comic books. *See* specific comic books
Computer matrix. *See* Matrix
Computers: anthropomorphic descrip-
    tions of, 13, 126–127; communication
    via, 71–72; computer hardware
    associated with penis length in
    advertisement, 51–52; computer
    networks about sex, 54–55; concealed
    and mysterious intricacy of, 102;
    cyberspace as feminine, 72–73; as
    defining technology of late twentieth

century, 39; and depthlessness, 43–44;
    feminine metaphors for, 72–73, 104,
    155; gendered metaphors for, 9–10,
    72–73, 104, 155; history of, 44–46;
    human brains compared with, 13,
    124–130; impact of, 44–46; jacking
    into cyberspace, 72–76; in *Mann and
    Machine*, 154–156; neural network-
    style computers, 21; and
    postmodernism, 39, 43–46; power of,
    100; predatory computer, 46; sex
    software for, 53–54, 80; sexuality
    associated with, 11–12, 50–79, 126,
    131–132; and terminal identity, 44; and
    warfare, 46. *See also* Electronic
    technology
Count Zero (Gibson), 31, 35–36, 42, 72
Crash (Ballard), 5–8, 12, 33, 161
CyberArts, 89–90
Cyberpunk comic book, 62, 63, 64, 65,
    77, 78
Cyberpunk fiction: and body obsoles-
    cence, 31–37; and collapse between
    fiction and reality, 32–33; and
    cyborg's status, 33–34; digital
    existence in, 13, 130–135; dystopian
    visions in, 11, 37, 72, 76; female
    characters in, 13, 135–145; human
    extinction in, 36–37; human psyche
    redefined in computer paradigm,
    130–135; and immortality, 76–77;
    jacking into cyberspace, 72–76;
    Landon's critique of, 144–145; male
    protagonists in, 72–76; mind/body
    dualism in, 31–32; misogyny in, 105,
    135–136; posthuman future in, 11,
    31–37; repressed memories and rage
    in, 13, 135–138, 141–144; sexual identity
    and sexuality in, 12, 36, 64–66, 140–144;
    superrich and quest for immortality
    in, 41–43; trivialization of history in,
    41; and uncertainty of human
    identity, 34–36; woman's revenge for
    sexual abuse in, 135–137
Cyberpunk game, 76
Cybersex. *See* Sexuality

Cyberspace (Stone), 82
Cyborgasm, 53
Cyborgs: androids compared with, 20;
armored-body imagery of, 108–109,
111; and bodiless sexuality, 62, 63, 64;
compared with human beings, 33–34;
corporeality intensified in, 51, 96;
dark side of culture of cyborgs, 133;
and death linked with eroticism,
59–62; definition of, 10, 18–19; female
cyborgs, 13, 114–117, 115, 116, 157; as
feminized and feminist figure, 66–67,
105, 129; Haraway's "Manifesto for
Cyborgs," 33–34, 66–67, 105;
hardware-interfaced cyborg, 19; and
immortality, 76–77; male cyborgs,
12–13, 95–124; in *Mann and Machine*,
14, 29, 30–31; Max Headroom, 96,
97–98; nudity of, 106–107; paradoxical
nature of, 77, 79; repressed memories
and rage of, 13, 135–144; and repro-
duction/destruction, 118–120;
RoboCop (character), 12, 13, *19*, 20,
31, 95, 98–99, 102, 108–111, *110*, 113,
129, 135, 137–138, 140; robots compared with, 20, 58; sexuality and
gender roles of, 59–62, 68–70, 77, 79,
102–108, 140; software-interfaced
cyborg, 19–20, 96; Terminator
(character), 12, *18*, 20, 30, 31, 32, 95,
96, 98–99, 102, 106–109, *107*, 108, 111–
114, *113*, 129, 140; and transgressed
boundaries, 58–59; types of, 19–20;
violence of, 95–96, 98–99, 106–114,
120–124; women characters in cyborg
films, 113–114, 138–139, *139*. *See also*
Machine-women

D'Alessandro, K.C., 3–4, 57
Death wish, 59
Defense Department, 81, 129
Defining technologies, 38, 39
De Landa, Manuel, 46
Delany, Samuel, 67
De l'Isle-Adam, Villiers, 148
Demon Seed, 119, 126

De Rougemont, Denis, 61–62
Dery, Mark, 55, 84, 138
Descartes, René, 16, 19, 28–29, 38–39, 49
Doane, Mary Ann, 102
Duke University, 29

Effinger, George Alec, 34, 42, 64, 66,
131–132
Electric Language (Heim), 85
Electronic Frontier Foundation, 82
Electronic technology: compared with
industrial technology, 4–5, 104–105;
computers associated with sexuality,
11–12, 50–79; concealed and mysterious intricacy of computers, 102;
gendered metaphors for computers,
9–10, 72–73, 104, 155; humans similar
to computers, 13, 124–130; impact of,
44–46; in *Mann and Machine*,
154–156; and postmodernism, 39,
43–46; and techno-eroticism, 4–5, 8,
10; virtual reality and erotic fantasies,
12, 80–94; and warfare, 46. *See also*
Computers; Cyborgs; Virtual reality
Elektra Assassin, 120, 136, 137
Eliminators, 30
Emotions: Minsky on, 30; rage of
patriarchal unconscious, 93–94;
repressed memories and rage in
cyborg films and cyberpunk fiction,
13, 135–144; versus reason in *Mann
and Machine*, 30–31
Emperor's New Mind, The (Penrose), 23
Empire of the Senseless (Acker), 136–137
ENIAC, 44–45, 46
Enlightenment philosophy, 18, 33, 34, 37
Ernst, Max, 109
Erotic fantasies, and virtual reality, 12,
80–94
Eroticism. *See* Sexuality; Techno-eroticism
Event Horizons, 55
Eve of Destruction, 13, 104, 114–117, *115*,
116, 135, 138, 147, 148, 157
Exile Kiss, The (Effinger), 34, 64, 131
Export, Valie, 49, 105
Exterminator, 30

Fascist ideology, 109, 111
Feminism: and cyberpunk fiction,
    135–136, 139–140; and cyborg as
    feminized and feminist figure, 66–67,
    105; definition of, 15; feminist critique
    of objectivity, 46–47; feminist critique
    of technology, 48; feminist science
    fiction, 12, 67, 105; and *Mann and
    Machine*, 158–161; nontechnophobic
    feminist positions, 49, 105, 155;
    poststructuralist feminism, 49
Fiction 2000 (Slusser and Shippey), 31
"Film Body" (Williams), 80
Films: erotic films transferred to CD-
    ROMs, 53; and homophobia, 99;
    television compared with, 97, 153;
    voyeuristic urge in development of,
    80–81, 148; *See also* specific films
Fire in the Sun, A (Effinger), 34, 42–43,
    64, 131
Fjermedal, Grant, 22
Forester, Tom, 44–45
Foster, Hal, 109
Foucault, Michel, 79
Frankenstein (Shelley), 24
Frankenstein theme, of robots, 101
Freud, Sigmund, 43, 59, 127, 135
Frude, Neil, 28
Future Sex, 52, 89

Galatea and Pygmalion myth, 29, 148
Galileo, 100
Gantz, John, 52, 126
Garb, Yaakov, 24–25
Gender: androgyny, 97; of computers,
    9–10, 72–73, 104, 155; contemporary
    crisis over, 48–49; in cyberpunk, 12,
    36, 64–66; cyberspace as feminine,
    72–73; of cyborgs, 68–70, 77, 79,
    102–108; definition of, 15; feminine
    metaphors for computers, 72–73, 104,
    155; fluidity of, in online environ-
    ment, 58; of machines, 9–10, 48, 51,
    104–105; in *Mann and Machine*, 14,
    149–150, 152–161; no gender in
    posthuman future, 67; in patriarchal

system, 49; and postmodernism, 85;
    power relations between the sexes in
    virtual sex, 89–94; in science fiction,
    12, 36, 64–67; and two-sex versus one-
    sex model, 103–104; and virtual
    reality, 85, 88; virtual reality as
    feminized subjectivity, 94
Gibson, William, 31, 35–36, 41–42, 57–58,
    62, 70–73, 76–77, 86, 131–132, 135, 136
Girl Who Was Plugged In, The
    (Tiptree), 35
Golem, Joseph, 28
Graziunas, Diana, 141
Greek myths, 28, 29
Griffin, Susan, 25
*GURPS Cyberpunk High-Tech Low-Life
    Roleplaying Sourcebook*, 76

Hahn, Roger, 100
Haraway, Donna, 33–34, 48, 49, 55–56,
    66–67, 105, 129, 141, 155
Hardboiled comic book, 120–124, 121, 123
Hardcore (Williams), 80
Harding, Sandra, 47
Hardware, 117, 118
Hardwired (Williams), 36, 66, 74–75,
    125, 134, 137
Hart, Lee, 51
Hartley, Nina, 24
Hayles, N. Katherine, 7, 47
Heim, Michael, 85–87, 88
High-Tech Society (Forester), 44
History, 40–41
Homophobia, 99
Hudak, Chris, 53
Human beings: and bodily obsolescence,
    23–27, 31–38; brain as machine, 39;
    brain compared with computers, 13,
    124–130; cyborgs compared with,
    33–34; Descartes' comparison of
    machines to, 16, 19, 38–39; dualities
    in human-centered universe, 33–34;
    Enlightenment philosophers on, 18,
    33, 34; machine-human relationship
    based on industrialization, 17–18;
    machine-human relationship in late

twentieth century, 18, 29, 55–56;
mind/body duality, 23, 31–32, 34, 49;
and posthuman future, 10–11, 18–49;
and terminal identity, 44; transmigration of human consciousness, 29–30;
as "Turing's Man," 18, 127; unique
characteristics of, 17–18. See also
Body; Brain; Sexuality
Humanoid automata, 28–29, 57, 100, 101
Huyssen, Andreas, 56–57

Immortality, 41–43, 76–77
Industrial technology: compared with
electronic technology, 4–5, 104–105;
and machine-human relationship,
17–18; techno-eroticism of, 3–5, 9–10;
violence associated with, 99–101. See
also Machines
In Our Own Image (Caudill), 21
Interface comic book, 68, 69, 70
International Spectrum, 51–52
Internet, 55
Italian futurism, 3

Jacking into cyberspace, 72–76
Jacobson, Linda, 89–90
Jameson, Fredric, 5, 34, 39, 40, 41, 87,
154–155
"Johnny Mnemonic" (Gibson), 136
Joy of Cybersex, The, 53
Joyrich, Lynne, 98

Kendrick, Walter, 55
Kroker, Arthur, 40
Kroker, Marilouise, 40

Lady El (Starlin and Graziunas), 13,
140–145
Landon, Brooks, 144–145
Lang, Fritz, 14
Laqueur, Thomas, 103
Laurel, Brenda, 89
Lawnmower Man, 83, 84, 91–94, 92, 93
Leary, Timothy, 135
LeGuin, Ursula, 12

Leibniz, Gottfried, 38, 85–86
L'Eve future (Tomorrow's Eve), 147, 148
Levy, Steven, 17–18, 21
Liquid Sky, 97
Love beyond Death (Binion), 62
Love in the Western World (de
Rougemont), 61–62
Lyotard, Jean-François, 17, 45–47, 67, 140

Machina Ex Dea (Rothschild), 48
Machines: brain as, 39; changes in,
during twentieth century, 39;
Descartes' comparison of human
beings to, 16, 19, 38–39; female
sexuality associated with, 56–57;
gendered and sexual metaphors for,
9–10, 48, 51, 56–57, 104; history of
view of, 100–101; human brain
compared with computers, 13;
machine-human relationship based
on industrialization, 17–18; machine-
human relationship in late twentieth
century, 18, 29, 55–56; mechano-
eroticism, 55; as mysterious and
magical, 100; violence associated
with, 99–101. See also Computers;
Cyborgs; Industrial technology
Machines Who Think (McCorduck), 21
Machine-women: eroticization of,
148–149; in late part of twentieth
century, 13–14; in L'Eve future
(Tomorrow's Eve), 147, 148; in Mann
and Machine, 14, 29, 30–31, 146–161;
in Metropolis, 14, 56, 56, 68, 150–151,
152, 157. See also Cyborgs
"MacPlaymates," 53
Madonna, 128
Making Sex (Laqueur), 103
Male Fantasies (Theweleit), 88, 109
"Manifesto for Cyborgs" (Haraway),
33–34, 66–67, 105
Mann and Machine: compared with
Metropolis, 13, 147, 150–157; contra-
dictory messages about gender roles
in, 14; danger of female sexuality in,

156–157; Eve's name in, 148; gender in, 149–150, 152–161; influences on, 147–148; and male desire to construct ideal woman, 29; Mann's reaction to Eve in, 149–150, 152–153; postmodernism of, 153–158; reason versus emotion in, 30–31; space in, 153; stills from, *150, 156*; technology in, 154–156; as television series, 146, 153; uncertain nature of Eve as android or cyborg, 147; visual style of, 153

Masturbation, 68, 70

Matrix, 59, 63, 68, 70, 140

Max Headroom (character), 96, 97–98

Max Headroom (television series), 97

McCaffery, Larry, 31

McCorduck, Pamela, 21

McIntyre, Vonda, 67

Mechanical women. *See* Machine-women

Mechano-eroticism, 55

Metropolis, 14, 56, *56*, 68, 99, 114, 120, 147, 150–152, *152*, 154–155, 157

Miami Vice, 147, 153

Michelson, Annette, 148

Milhon, Jude, 89

Military, and computers, 46

Miller, Frank, 120, 138

Mills, Stephanie, 24

Mind/body duality, 23, 31–32, 34, 49, 126

"Mind Is a Leaking Rainbow" (Stenger), 88

Mindplayers (Cadigan), 134

Minsky, Marvin, 26, 30, 39, 129–130, 132

Mobile Robot Laboratory, Carnegie Mellon University, 22

Mona Lisa Overdrive (Gibson), 31, 72, 136

Mondo 2000, 7, 52, 89, 94

Moravec, Hans, 21–22, 29, 32–33, 41, 49, 67, 96, 126, 130, 132

Multinational capitalism, 41

Naked Computer, The (Rochester and Gantz), 52, 126

Neale, Steven, 99

Networks about sex, 54–55

Neural network, 21

Neuromancer (Gibson), 31, 42, 72–74, 86, 131, 136

NewMedia, 55

Nixon, Nicola, 72–73, 105, 135

Nudity, 106–107

Objectivity, feminist critique of, 47–48

O'Brien, Mark, 25–26

Offray de la Mettrie, Julien, 39

"Overdrawn at the Memory Bank" (Varley), 133–134

Palac, Lisa, 89

Panic bodies, in postmodernist consumer society, 40

Patriarchy: in cyborg films, 114–120; definition of, 14–15; and fear of female sexuality, 56–57, 114–118, 147, 157–159; gender difference in, 49, 68; in *Mann and Machine*, 158–160; in *Metropolis*, 151–152; mind/body duality in, 49; rage of patriarchal unconscious, 93–94; in science and technology, 47–48; in virtual reality, 85–87, 88

Pauline, Mark, 27

Penley, Constance, 30, 66, 97, 106

Penrose, Roger, 23

Pierce, John J., 135

Plato, 38, 85

Pleasure principle, 59

Pornography, 55, 68, 70, 89–90

Postmodern Condition, The (Lyotard), 45–46

Postmodernism: and computers, 39, 43–46; consumer society, 40; definition of, 39–40; and delegitimation of scientific knowledge, 46–47; and depthlessness, 43–44; and gender identity, 85; of *Mann and Machine*, 153–158; and multinational capitalism, 41; obsession with simulacra, 130; and

posthuman age, 41; space and time
in, 40–41, 43–44, 87, 153, 154; and
superrich, 41–43; and uncertainty,
67–68
Poststructuralism, 49, 130
Predatory computer, 46
Primate Visions (Haraway), 48
Primatology, 48
Pygmalion and Galatea myth, 29, 148

R.U.R., 101
Racism, 48, 135
Re-Animator, 30
Reproduction/destruction, 118–120
Rheingold, Howard, 82–83
Rice, Anne, 128
Rich, Frank, 128
RoboCop (character), 12, 13, 19, 20, 31,
95, 98–99, 102, 108–111, 110, 113, 129,
135, 137–138, 140, 155
RoboCop (film), 19, 31, 108–111, 110,
113, 147, 155
RoboCop 2, 120
RoboCop versus the Terminator, 30, 120,
137–138
Robots: cyborgs compared with, 20, 58;
as dangerous entities in fiction, 101;
eroticization of female robots,
148–149; female robot in *Metropolis*,
14, 56, 56, 150–151, 152; origin of
term, 101. *See also* Cyborgs;
Machine-women
Rochester, Jack, 52, 126
Ronell, Avital, 49, 105
Ronin, 120
Ross, Andrew, 66, 105, 136
Rothschild, Joan, 48
Rucker, Rudy, 31–32, 76–77
Russ, Joanna, 12, 67
Russian Terminator, The, 30

Saenz, Michael, 54, 80, 82, 89
Schank, Roger C., 127–128
Schwab, Gabriele, 133
Schwarzenegger, Arnold, 111, 112
Science: delegitimation of scientific

knowledge, 46–47; feminist critique
of objectivity, 47–48; history of, 100
Science fiction: Ballard's *Crash*, 5–8, 12,
33; female cyborgs in, 13; feminist
science fiction, 12, 67, 105; gender in,
12, 36, 64–67; Moravec on importance of, 32–33; posthuman future in,
11, 31–37; reproduction/destruction in,
118–120; simulated life portrayed in,
23–24. *See also* Cyberpunk fiction;
and specific authors and titles
Secret Museum, The (Kendrick), 55
Seraphim comic book, 137
Sex (Madonna), 128
Sexes, two-sex versus one-sex model of,
103–104
Sex software, 53–54, 80
Sexual identity. *See* Gender; Sexuality
Sexuality: anonymity of computer sex,
58; bodiless sexuality, 61–64, 68–70,
83–84; cerebral sexuality, 68–70;
computer hardware associated with
penis length in advertisement, 51–52;
computer networks on, 54–55;
computers associated with, 11–12,
50–79, 126, 131–132; in cyberpunk
fiction, 140–144; cybersex in advertising, 52–53; cyberspace as feminine,
72–73; of cyborgs, 59–62, 68–70, 77,
79, 102–108; death linked with, 59–62,
128; digital sex, 53–56; of female
robots, 56, 68, 148–149, 150–151, 152;
female sexuality associated with
machines, 56–57; high-tech sex toys,
52; jacking into cyberspace, 72–76; of
machines, 51, 104–105; masturbation,
68, 70; mechano-eroticism, 55; in
Metropolis, 56, 68, 150–151, 152;
patriarchal fear of female sexuality,
56–57, 114–118, 147, 157–159; power
relations between the sexes in virtual
sex, 89–94; sex software, 53–54, 80;
and two-sex versus one-sex model,
103–104; violence as displacement of
male sexuality, 99; virtual reality and
erotic fantasies, 12, 80–94

Sexy Robot (Sorayama), 148–149
Shadows of the Mind (Penrose), 23
Shaper/Mechanist series (Sterling), 36–37
Sheldon, Alice B., 35
Shelley, Mary, 23–24
Shippey, Tom, 31
Simulated life: and adaptation for survival, 27; critics of, 22–23; enthusiasm for, 21–22; history of interest in, 28–29; in science fiction, 11, 23–24, 31–38; scientific work on, 16–17, 21–23, 32–33
"Sleazenet," 54
Slusser, George, 31
Sobchack, Vivian, 7, 44, 90–91, 106–107, 118–119
Society of Mind, The (Minsky), 30
Software (Rucker), 31–32
Sony television advertisement, 34–35
Sorayama, Hajime, 148–149
Space: in *Mann and Machine*, 153; in *Metropolis*, 153–154; in postmodern society, 40, 41, 43–44, 87
Sperminator, 30
Starhawk, 23, 24
Starlin, Jim, 140–141
Star Trek: The Next Generation, 37, 59–61
Stenger, Nicole, 88
Sterling, Bruce, 27, 36–37, 102
Stone, Allucquere Rosanne, 82, 94
Stone Age sculpture, 8–9
Storming the Reality Studio (McCaffery), 31
Survival Research Laboratories, 27

Tales of the New Teen Titans, 135
Teaching Technology from a Feminist Perspective (Rothschild), 48
Techno-eroticism: and the automobile, 4, 5–8; in Ballard's *Crash*, 5–8; and cyborgs, 10; and electronic technology, 4–5, 8, 10; and gendered metaphors for machines, 9–10; industrial-age techno-eroticism, 3–5,

9–10; and Italian futurism, 3; and Stone Age sculpture, 8–9. *See also* Sexuality
Technology: defining technologies, 38, 39; definition of, 15; feminist critique of, 48; post-modern technology, 39; sex and gender in description of, 9–10, 48, 51, 56–57, 104–105; violence associated with, 99–101. *See also* Computers; Electronic technology; Industrial technology
Technology and Culture, 51
Teledildonics, 82–83
Television: film compared with, 97, 153; *Mann and Machine* as television series, 146, 153; Max Headroom (character), 96, 97–98; viewing of, as sacred, 70–71
Terminal identity, 44
Terminal Identity (Bukatman), 31
Terminator (character), 12, 18, 20, 31, 32, 95, 96, 98–99, 102, 106–109, 107, 108, 111–114, 113, 129, 140, 155
Terminator, The (comic book), 30
Terminator, The (film), 18, 30, 31, 32, 106–109, 113, 138–139, 155
Terminator 2: Judgment Day, 30, 96, 107–108, 107, 108, 109, 112–114, 113, 138–139, 139, 155
Tetsuo: The Iron Man, 117
Tetsuo II: The Body Hammer, 117–118
Theweleit, Klaus, 88, 93–94, 109, 111, 117, 118
"Throbnet," 54
Tierney, John, 8–9
Time, in postmodern society, 40–41
Tiptree, James, Jr., 35
Tomas, David, 19
Tomorrow Makers: A Brave New World of Living-Brain Machines (Fjermedal), 22
Total Recall, 111
Transmigration of human consciousness, 29–30, 32
Tristan and Iseult legend, 61
"Turing's Man," 18, 127

Turing's Man, 38
Turkle, Sherry, 18, 125, 126, 127
"Twenty Evocations" (Sterling), 37
"Twenty Minutes into the Future," 96,
    97–98
2001: A Space Odyssey, 126

University of Pennsylvania, 44

"Vamp and the Machine, The"
    (Huyssen), 56
Varley, John, 67, 133–134
Vaucanson, Jacques de, 28
Venus figurines, 8–9
Vindicator, The, 30
Violence: of cyborgs, 95–96, 98–99,
    106–114, 120–124; as displacement of
    male sexuality, 99; technology
    associated with, 99–101
"Virginity of Astronauts, The"
    (Sobchack), 118–119
Virtual Light (Gibson), 41, 42, 57–58,
    70–71
Virtual Reality (Rheingold), 82–83
Virtual reality (VR): and blasting away
    of gender and sexual constraints, 88;
    and central clearing house, 87;

central metaphors, 88; description of,
    81–82; and erotic fantasies, 12, 80–94;
    as feminized subjectivity, 94; and
    gender definition, 85, 88; Heim on,
    85–87; history of, 81; and lack of
    concern over social realities, 91; in
    Lawnmower Man, 83, 84, 91–94, 92,
    93; patriarchal virtual reality, 85–87,
    88; power relations between the sexes
    in virtual sex, 89–94; Stenger on, 88
"Virtual Valerie," 53–54, 80
VR. *See* Virtual reality

War in the Age of Intelligent Machines
    (De Landa), 46
Warfare, and electronic technology, 46
Weedon, Chris, 14–15
Weird Science, 29, 119–120, 148
When Gravity Fails (Effinger), 34, 64,
    131, 132
Whole Earth Review, 24
"Whorehouse," 53
Whose Science? Whose Knowledge?
    (Harding), 47
Williams, Linda, 68, 80
Williams, Walter Jon, 36, 66, 74–75,
    134, 137